S0-BYP-749

WITHDRAWN

DATE DUE

GAYLORD			PRINTED IN U.S.A.

THE ROLE OF THEOLOGY IN THE UNIVERSITY

 CONTEMPORARY COLLEGE THEOLOGY SERIES

GENERAL EDITORS: J. FRANK DEVINE, S.J.
BOSTON COLLEGE

RICHARD W. ROUSSEAU, S.J.
FAIRFIELD UNIVERSITY

THE ROLE OF THEOLOGY IN THE UNIVERSITY is one of the volumes in the introductory section in this series.

The Role of Theology
in the University

DANIEL CALLAHAN

WILLIAM SCOTT, S.J.

F. X. SHEA, S.J.

THE BRUCE PUBLISHING COMPANY / MILWAUKEE

CARL A. RUDISILL LIBRARY
LENOIR RHYNE COLLEGE

IMPRIMI POTEST:
    LEO J. McGOVERN, S.J.
    Vice Provincial

    CORNELIUS J. CARR, S.J.
    Provincial

NIHIL OBSTAT:
    JOHN A. SCHULIEN, S.T.D.
    Censor librorum

IMPRIMATUR:
    ✠ WILLIAM E. COUSINS
    Archbishop of Milwaukee
    July 13, 1967

230
C 13 n
61983
June 1968

The *Nihil obstat* and *Imprimatur* are a declaration that a book or pamphlet is considered to be free from doctrinal or moral error. It is not implied that those who have granted the *Nihil obstat* and *Imprimatur* agree with the contents, opinions, or statements expressed.

Library of Congress Catalog Card Number: 67–28215

© 1967 THE BRUCE PUBLISHING COMPANY
MADE IN THE UNITED STATES OF AMERICA

Acknowledgments

We are grateful to the following for permission to cite copyrighted materials:

The editors of *The Commonweal* and George Lindbeck, for citations from Dr. Lindbeck's article, "The Thrust of 'Progressive' Catholicism," *The Commonweal*, October 18, 1963, and John Ratte, for citations from Mr. Ratte's article, "The Specter of Modernism," *The Commonweal*, July 23, 1965;

The editors of *Continuum* and Dr. Rosemary Reuther, for citations from Dr. Reuther's "Loisy: History and Commitment" in *Continuum* (Summer, 1965), and Dr. Francis O'Connor, for citations from Dr. O'Connor's "Tyrrell: The Nature of Revelation" from the same issue of *Continuum*; Harcourt, Brace, and World, Inc., New York, for lines from T. S. Eliot's *East Coker;*

Hawthorn Books, Inc., New York, for excerpts from M.-D. Chenu's *Is Theology a Science?* in The Twentieth Century Encyclopedia of Catholicism, Copyright 1959 by Hawthorn Books, Inc.;

Helicon Press, Baltimore, for excerpts from Yves M.-J. Congar's *Power and Poverty in the Church* and from Karl Rahner's *Theological Investigations,* Volume I;

The Macmillan Company, New York, for lines from *Collected Poems* by William Butler Yeats. Copyright 1934 by The Macmillan Company, renewed 1962 by Bertha George Yeats;

Thomas Nelson and Sons, New York and Edinburgh, for material from Hans Küng's *Structures of the Church;*

New Directions Publishing Corporation, New York, for lines from Ezra Pound's *Personae,* Copyright 1926, 1954 by Ezra Pound.

Sheed & Ward, Inc., New York, for material from *Newman the Theologian* by J. -H. Walgrave. © Geoffrey Chapman, Ltd., 1960.

Editors' Introduction

The Contemporary College
Theology Series

This series begins with the presupposition that theology is necessary. It is necessary if Christian intelligence is to search for meaning in its dialogue with God, man, and the world. Since Christian intelligence is not the exclusive possession of the theological specialist or the cleric, the search must be carried on in all those areas of life, secular as well as religious, including the college situation, where meaning is to be found.

This search is a peaceful one, for in some mysterious way it has already achieved its goal: the vision of faith and the fullness of love. Still it remains a relentless and universal search. Its inner certainty must radiate out not only to the edges of the mind but also into the farthest recesses of the world. We could call it "lay" theology, but this word seems too pale a description for such an exciting enterprise of the Christian life.

In view of this the editors of this series are convinced that new questions had to be asked, new structures created, and new books written. These books would be neither catechetical nor apologetic. They would be purely and simply theological. The primary audience would be believers, but all thinking men would find them useful. In scope they would be broad enough to ensure perspective. They would be scholarly enough to be intellectually relevant. They would avoid pedantry. In short they would try to present a rich and deep understanding of Christian revelation in such a way that today's college students would be able to respond with a Christian faith and life that are both culturally mature and scientifically precise. Finally the authors of these books would be, for the most part, teachers in colleges and universities where much of the contemporary theological dialogue is now going on.

The series falls into four parts: biblical, historical, ecclesial, and ethical. The divisions were not predetermined by the editors. They follow the shape of the most vigorous theological work now being done.

The books in the biblical section are intended to go beyond the traditional treatment of Bible history and the now familiar perspectives of salvation history. They concentrate on various books of the Bible. Their method has been especially designed for college work. Tentatively it might be called "exegetical theology." Every verse is not considered after the fashion of a commentary, nor are narratives developed as a biography, nor is there any attempt to create large theological syntheses. Rather the individual books are studied in chronological sequence; key passages are treated in detail and the rest are summarized. At the same time some attention is paid to the growing theological synthesis.

Since scholastic theology is already represented by individual works and sets of textbooks, the books in our historical section study dogmatic questions from a developmental point of view. In this way the editors hope to make the college students more aware of the great wealth of theological thinking that recent historico-theological studies have uncovered. This method which is more inductive than deductive should happily coincide with the thought processes of the college student. The three basic poles for synthesis are: God, Christ, and Man. In each area the historical development will be studied and a significant number of basic source texts presented. The problems raised in these studies will range all the way from Augustinian pessimism to Teilhardian optimism.

The textbooks for the third part of the series will deal with issues of great contemporary importance. They will examine questions discussed by the Second Vatican Council. As the name implies, ecclesial theology must first concern itself with the Church, what the Church knows herself to be, as expressed in the insights of the new *Constitution on the Church* and with the more significant of the Church's allied concerns: other world religions, American Protestantism, its history, its motivating forces and spirit, and finally the new sacramental theology so enriched by the many magnificent liturgical advances. All of this growth has brought a wider and deeper appreciation of the nature of the Roman Catholic Church and her relationship rooted in understanding and love with the whole world.

The fourth and final section of the series is devoted explicitly to Christian moral response. The editors subscribe to the position that the proper place for the Catholic college or university to examine ethical questions is in a revelational rather than in a purely philosophical context. In addition to the "virtue" divisions of the *Summa* or the classic moral theology text, designed primarily for confessors, there is a need and a place for a "Christian ethics" that reflects the new insight which both biblical and dogmatic theology can provide. These books will strive to be openly Christian in spirit, eclectic in approach, up to date in scholarship, and will address themselves to those ethical problems which are most real to the modern American mind.

Finally, the editors would like to express their thanks to all those whose interest, advice, and cooperation have made this series possible. They are especially grateful to Mr. William May of The Bruce Publishing Company, who not only initiated the project and sustained it through the inevitable disappointments and complications, but contributed so much of his editorial skill to its final shape. To the individual authors who so graciously added to their heavy burden of academic responsibility by undertaking these books, we can only express the hope that their share in the shaping and influencing of the American Catholic community of today and of tomorrow will be far more meaningful to them than any meager thanks of ours.

The Editors,
Rev. J. Frank Devine, S.J., Boston College
Rev. Richard W. Rousseau, S.J., Fairfield University

Contents

I

Theology and the Layman

By Daniel Callahan

THE first thing one notices about theology is that its cash value is slight. There are few if any businesses which require that a man or woman know theology; most could not care less. No company president is likely to hand out promotions because one's understanding of the Trinity is marked by knowledge and insight. No medical school is likely to award degrees because of an advanced perception into the central Christian truth that man is made in the image of God. Law cases are not won, nor clients gained, by an ability to be articulate about Christian truth. The fact that one may, in college, have taken three or four years of theology is not going to interest most prospective employers at all; nor will it be of much interest to the admission boards of most graduate or professional schools.

These are not its only limitations. Theology will not necessarily enable one to win friends and influence people. It will not make one

1

witty, will not improve one's appearance, will not enhance one's conversational ability, will not lead to a wider circle of friends. As if these limitations were not enough, theology can be extremely dull, requiring sustained effort over a long period of time, demanding hard thought, meditation, and speculation on abstract and difficult subjects. But at least, one might reply, theology does, after all, give one a tidy, certain set of truths — isn't that something? "Tidy," "certain" — no, not tidy, rarely certain. For theology too is a groping science, an approximation of the truth, an approach to the truth, a wrestling with truth. If one wants a neatly drawn blueprint of the truth, he had better look elsewhere. Theology is not a first-grade catechism with footnotes; its probings can rarely be memorized.

Viewed from almost every practical vantage point, then, theology has little to recommend it. Well, what good is it? To answer this question, it is necessary to observe, first, the world in which we live. When we look at that world, we see many things. We see nations struggling against each other, fighting over border markers and ideologies, trade and alliances, food and land. We see one nation living in affluence, another living in poverty. We see the threat of a nuclear war — or, if we live to a ripe old age, the prospect of death from cancer, coronaries, or one of the innumerable other ways of expiring in an unoriginal fashion. We see unemployment, cyclical economic flux, labor strife, and racial antagonisms, class warfare, and garden-variety nastiness and hate. It is not for nothing that ours has been called an "age of anxiety."

There is a form of religion which has an answer to this anxiety. Let us just call it popular religion, the religion of inspirational literature, heartwarming sermons, spiritual pep talks. This religion is shared by many, crossing credal barriers with consummate ease. It is a religion marked by an emphasis on faith — any faith. Have faith, this religion urges, because man needs something to hold on to. Have faith, because faith is better than doubt and uncertainty; faith makes for happy, contented people; the man of faith will have a good feeling inside. Going hand in hand with this faith in faith, popular religion likes to argue that the stability of society depends upon men of faith, strong and upright in their convictions. Take away faith, popular religion says, and what do you get: recessions, suicides, drunkenness, juvenile delinquency, broken homes — and on and on. In short, faith works: happier people, greener grass, lower prison and welfare budgets. The one thing that popular religion does not recommend very vigorously is hard thinking; for sometimes thinking leads to anxiety, and doubts, and problems. Better to wave the magic wand of "faith" over these troubles and put them out of mind. Popular religion looks for security of mind, mental and emotional peace at any price; it matters little whether one has a grasp of truth — what does matter is that one be at ease.

It would be a mistake to think that this form of religion has had no influence on the Church. Naturally, the Catholic will not be prone to say that just any old faith at all will do, so long as one has some kind of faith. He should at least know that God is the Person to whom he relates in faith. Nonetheless, it is perfectly possible for the Catholic to look upon his faith as a kind of crutch. All he has to do is to begin thinking only about the utility of faith: how it provides a haven from the storms of life (for is it not said that "there are no atheists in fox-holes?"); how it gives one a magic key to everlasting life (and we all want to live forever, don't we?); how it provides a prop for the laws by which society maintains its stability (don't our guardians of civic virtue tell us that the churchgoer makes a better citizen?). Besides these pragmatic reasons for "having faith," there are others, perhaps peculiar to Catholics. There is the fear of eternal damnation for those who have abandoned the faith (when this theme is stressed incessantly, it is all too easy to decide that one had better stop thinking and just hold fast). There is the fear of cutting oneself off from one's believing friends, from one's parents, from one's teachers (for those with a bent for conformity, this is indeed a powerful inducement to retain an unexamined faith). Then of course there is sheer laziness (for some, faith appears the easier course, demanding much less effort than a probing skepticism).

Catholics are hardly immune from the temptation to think in these terms. Let it be admitted that there is much about Catholicism which can, for some, act as an inducement to a mechanical, ritualistic religion. If one is not careful, one may begin to look upon the sacraments as routine, magical acts, requiring nothing more from the recipient than going through the proper motions. If one is not careful, one may begin to think of God as a kindly old-man-with-a-beard, good only for bailing us out when we get in trouble on earth. If one is not careful, one can come to believe that abstaining from meat on Friday is more important than loving one's neighbor. The great glory of law and ritual properly understood is that they can provide a genuine stability and unity for our religion. Improperly understood, however, they can be the seedbed of hypocrisy and evasion, providing the illusion of religion without its substance.

Christianity has its enemies in the modern world; of that there can be no doubt. But far more numerous than its enemies are those men of goodwill perplexed by what they see of the Christianity about them. They have heard it said that Christians are supposed to be men of charity; but they find it difficult to see tangible signs of this charity. (They can, of course, see Christians going to church on Sunday, but that is a rather different matter.) They have heard it said that Christians are men who renounce materialism, but to judge from the evidence this renunciation has only to do with philosophical materialism. Christians, it turns out, can be just as attached to practical materialism as the most dedicated hedonist. They have heard it said that Christianity is a religion for all times and for all cultures, but what they too often observe is that Christians seem to love the glorious, romantic past more than the imperfect present. It is hardly any wonder, then, that many nonbelievers will think the Christian is nothing but a fraud. The dramatist George Bernard Shaw once said that "the only trouble with Christianity is that it has never been tried." Another critic of Christianity cynically observed that "faith is the ability to convince oneself of what one knows to be false." The Marxists have claimed that "religion is the opiate of the people." Some existentialists have asserted that the Christian does not have the courage to assert his freedom, to stand on his own two feet as an independent, autonomous person. One may dismiss these observations as evidence of ill will or utter ignorance – but if one looks at the actual manifestations of Christianity in the world, and not just at its principles, one would be forced to hesitate. The evidence is, at best, mixed.

The Christian should be disturbed by this evidence. There was once a time, at least in the Western world, when Christianity held sway, when to be a civilized man was to be a Christian. During this long span of centuries, ranging from the early Middle Ages until perhaps the nineteenth century, the Christian had to give comparatively little thought to the kind of witness to Christ he bore in the world. After all, the world he knew was already Christian. He could afford to be complacent, and often he was just that. There was no culture on earth which could call Christendom to account, or none at least that the average Christian knew much about. Yet with the Enlightenment and the Industrial Revolution of the seventeenth and eighteenth centuries, the ground was being prepared for the breakup of Christendom. With the rise of the proletariat and the emergence of secular ideologies in the nineteenth century this breakup began to be a fact. By the middle of the twentieth century, men could already begin speaking of a "post-Christian era." For by then the great cultural, political, and theological synthesis which made up Western Christendom had all but ceased to exist. No longer could Christianity depend upon the force of social conformity to sustain its moral principles and its understanding of man's ultimate destiny. No longer could Christianity depend upon special favor and protection from the State. No longer could Christianity feel complacent and triumphant. Communism was one threat, Fascism another, secularism still another. Regardless of the direction in which one looked it had become clear that Christianity, after centuries of relative security and dominance, was once again thrown back on its spiritual resources alone. Some have bemoaned this great historical development; others have been indifferent; still others rejoiced — including many Christians who have come to believe that Christianity paid too great a spiritual price for its cultural dominance.

One way or another, however, the consequences of this change are enormous. For one thing, we live in a pluralistic age, an age in which many religions coexist in the same state, each normally protected by law. This means that, more than ever in the past, the Catholic is very much on his own. He must know how to live among men who do not share his beliefs. He must know how to do without those once-sustaining social mores which made it comparatively easy for his forefathers to practice their religion. He must know how to live in a world where there is no moral or religious consensus. He must know, in short, how to be a self-sustaining, self-directing person, one who knows how to resist the pressures of society, the inclination to blind conformity, and the temptation to seal religion off from life.

Much has been made in our day of "secularism," a word which does not mean so much a conscious, deliberate rejection of God, but rather a practical attitude toward life which acts as if man had only this world and no other, as if his terrestrial life was all that mattered. No doubt there is much secularism about; it is in the air we breathe. But it may well be doubted whether our age is any worse off in this respect than others. Whether more or less, however, it is impossible to build a religious life simply on the grounds that secularism is an evil and needs to be fought. Christians ought to have more positive goals than that.

Let us look at two possible goals: self-respect for one's natural dignity and the transformation of the world in Christ. Take the matter of one's natural dignity. As suggested above, the Christian is reproached, often justly, for fraudulent behavior: he talks Christian principles but acts like everyone else. He is a hypocrite; or worse, he doesn't really believe in his principles in the first place. Not only does he attempt to defraud the world, he seems willing to defraud himself. These are serious charges, far more devastating in their own way than those older attacks on Christianity which stressed, for instance, a supposed incompatibility between science and religion, or the impossibility of proving the existence of God. The new charge, in sum, is that not even "Christians" believe in Christianity. Another way of putting this is to say that Christians are dishonest: dishonest with the world and dishonest with themselves.

Our instinct as Christians will be to reject the charge of dishonesty, vehemently denying that we do not believe what we profess. Unfortunately, we cannot just dismiss the evidence the non-Christian sees about him; it exists and it is our burden. And how many of us, if we candidly take stock of our own belief, could really say that our faith is perfect? How many of us could say that nothing more than a love of God motivates our conformity to the Church? How many of us could confidently assert that we have courageously examined our faith and that it is free of motives of social conformity, fear of parental disfavor, and a timid unwillingness to face anxiety-producing problems and conflicts? How many of us, satisfied with a front of respectable piety, have willingly tolerated the presence within ourselves of a ritualistic, unthinking nod to the truths of Christianity?

These are unpleasant questions, each of them bringing into focus our integrity as human beings. But they are the kinds of questions the Christian must put to himself if he is to be worthy of his dignity as a person. It is perfectly possible for him to ignore them: he can obey the commandments of the Church, memorize the formulas his teachers put before him, be respectful toward the clergy and religious. If he does these things, no one will complain about him. He will be commended as a "good Catholic." But he can still be a fraud in terms of his inner life of mind and spirit: by failing to think, to put hard questions to himself, to demand honesty and integrity in his religious life. The Church has always stressed that Christian faith, which is a gift of God, must be a freely accepted faith. The Church has also taught that it is a rational, intelligent faith, not just a blind leap into the dark. It is a faith meant to enhance our reason, to raise our natural dignity as human beings to a new level of life and love. Yet this will not happen if we allow ourselves to be intellectual and moral automatons, floating on the tide of superficial piety and action. Worse than this, we will sooner or later come to realize that we have lived a life of partial falsehood. We will know we have settled for less than full integrity. We will know we have mouthed statements and beliefs whose meaning we have never taken the trouble to comprehend. We will know we have pledged our loyalty to a Church and God whose meaning we have not tried to fathom. We will know that we have put our difficulties of faith off into some corner of our mind, unwilling to explore and resolve them. If the non-Christian, in such a case, calls us a fraud, he will be right. To live a Christian life of intellectual and human integrity, then, ought to be one positive goal of the Christian.

Another goal should be the transformation of the world in Christ. To what are we called as Christians? We are called to live a life of love in Christ. We are called to prepare ourselves for our ultimate destiny, which is union with God. We are called to carry on Christ's work in the world: the work of redemption of man and matter. We are *not* told to run from the world; we are called to live in the world in a new way, a way in which the passion, death, and glorious resurrection of Christ are made efficacious and meaningful for all men. We must, in all we do, be witnesses to the love and truth which Christ brought to mankind.

Here is a dynamic mission for the Christian. It is not enough for the Christian to cultivate only his own spiritual garden. It is not enough for him just to keep the commandments of God and the Church. These are only the minimal requirements of a full Christian life. We are called to much more: called to a life of service, of struggle, of growth, of honesty. But that much Christians have always been called to. Today, however, there are some additional requirements. We live during a moment in history when the world is undergoing great changes. They can be seen on all sides: the emergence of the underdeveloped nations, the proliferation of nuclear weapons, the changes in community values, the presence of automation and cybernation, vast affluence juxtaposed to great poverty — and on and on. The situation of religion in such a world will inevitably be affected by these changes. Coming hard on the heels of the breakup of Christendom as a set of values and a culture common to the Western world, the Church now finds itself in a radically different relationship to the world. Men do not listen to the Church as they once did. Where the Church was once the pre-eminent force in the Western world it is now taken by men to be only one more institution; interesting, perhaps; colorful, to be sure; impressive in its size and long history, indubitably. But *relevant?* On this question, men will be uncertain. Some will flatly say no. Others will be doubtful. Still others will say: well, possibly. There is no unanimity. For one thing, Christianity has lost its power to stimulate the imagination of many, many people. Its place has been taken by politics, by ideologies, by popular culture, by the arts, by science, by technology. For another, Christianity itself has by no means clarified its own thinking on the nature of the contemporary world: some Christians want a return to the old order of things; they pine for a simpler world, one in which Christians held sway. Others want the Church to continue doing what it has always done, contenting itself only with the private spiritual needs of its adherents. Still others want the Church to radically change, stripping itself of everything that bears the marks of other eras. To add to these disagreements within the Church, the disunity of Christianity poses another obstacle. When Catholics and Protestants still have great difficulty communicating and cooperating with each other, when many old enmities remain, then all of the churches are that much more weakened in facing their common problems.

To say that all of this is confusing, troublesome, a source of anxiety is to say the obvious. What can be done about it? One cannot just go out and, hocus-pocus, make men listen. Nor can the Church just convene the bishops, let them talk for a time, and then issue manifestos to the world. This is not to say the Church cannot and must not try to make men listen. Nor is it to deny the value of the bishops' meeting in Council to grapple with the perplexities of our era. Rather, it is to recognize that the problem of the contemporary relevance of Christ and of the Church must be the concern of the whole Church. Sometimes it is tempting to think that brilliant theologians alone can bring Christianity a new vitality; or that a well-trained body of lay leaders working hand in hand with the bishops and clergy could well manage the Church's problems. But this will not do: the task of the Church today is so vast that only the total Church can adequately deal with it.

But no sooner does one speak of the "total Church" than it becomes obvious that the laity's role is crucial. The reason for this does not lie only in the fact that the laity are far more numerous than the clergy. Instead, it lies in the more important fact that the Church's presence in the world comes down to the presence of the laity in the world. To be sure, the Church is present in the world by virtue of its church edifices, its schools, its orphanages, its hospitals, its charitable projects; it is also present in its priests, nuns, and brothers. These things the world can see; they cannot be missed. But the Church the world sees much more closely is the Church as it manifests itself in the Catholic people. The institutions of the Church, its buildings and symbols, are seen mainly at a distance; the Church the world rubs shoulders with is the lay Catholic. And of course he is the Church every bit as much as the popes, bishops, and priests. The Church is the whole people of God, not just those who are pastors and teachers in the Church. That great insight of our day means, at the very least, one thing of great importance: no one who is a member of the Church can claim that he has no responsibility for the Church; nor can he claim that the problems of the Church are someone else's problems; nor can he claim that he is not a "theologian" or a "scholar" or a "specialist" and hence can be excused from thinking deeply about the Church. To be meaningful to the world, to speak fully and persuasively to the world, the voice of the whole Church must be heard; that is, the voice of the hierarchy, the clergy, and the laity together.

It is at this point that theology becomes vital for the layman. Once it is seen that the Church is as much the responsibility of the layman as that of anyone else, then it becomes necessary that the layman understand the Church, his faith, and the meaning of the revelation of Christ. A responsible person is one who recognizes the obligations and possibilities of his situation, of his dignity as a person, and of his need to contribute to the good of the whole. One can, naturally, choose not to be responsible: our society is large enough and diverse enough to hide those who choose to evade the higher demands of integrity and responsibility. No one is likely to know about the evasion; and it is simple enough to feign a life of responsibility. But once again we are back to fraud: the irresponsible, the unthinking life cheats both the person himself and his society — and it cheats the Church.

But where must responsibility start? Surely it must at least start with a steadfast desire to be responsible. Yet desire is not enough; reason must attend this desire and give it direction. And reason must be accompanied by imagination, speculation, and contemplation. It is impossible to be responsible without an understanding, on the one hand, of those mysteries of the Christian dispensation which provide the spiritual ground on which we stand; and, on the other, of that world of time, matter, culture, and history in which man is immersed. Of necessity, these understandings will always be inadequate. The mysteries of Christian truth will always remain mysteries, penetrable only in part. The world in which we live, ever changing, will only give up its secrets slowly and in a fragmentary way. Perhaps harder still is the task of relating our understanding of Christian truth to our natural perceptions and insights into the world. But do we really have any choice other than to try?

We live, for instance, in a complicated political society, shot through with people of different values, different backgrounds, different political orientations. How are we to relate our understanding of the Christian message to these complex human facts? We may say, for instance, that all men are made in the image of God. But how do we relate this truth to racial integration? On one level the answer seems easy enough: if all men are made in the image of God, and all alike are children of God, then it follows that society cannot condone political inequalities based on the color of a man's skin. That is a good answer — as far as it goes. But what happens when one has to frame laws? What kinds of laws should be passed? Toward what goal should the laws aim? Here one passes into the messy, nasty details of reality; and, once immersed, clarity and certainty seem difficult to come by. For the Christian to speak to these details, it will not suffice to shout about man's being made in God's image: that is an abstract principle, a truth — it does not provide a program for political action, nor the passage of laws, nor the correction of economic and employment problems. What is called for here is a deep penetration into the meaning of man's relationship to God and, in the light of that relationship, of his bond with other human beings. The truth that "man is made in the image of God" must take on depth and scope; it must become more than an axiom, more than an abstract proposition. But that means more questions will have to be asked.

Toward what should a Christian work in society? What should the word "society" mean for a Christian? What should be the value and place of secular institutions: the State, the culture, the political process, the economic mechanisms? Again, we have hard, hard questions on our hands, questions which will not be solved by platitudes or slogans. We need, then, a theology of society: an understanding of society, that is, which attempts to relate our understanding of God's will for men to those temporal structures which intimately affect man's temporal, and ultimately, spiritual lot. But to undertake this task requires a grasp of the Incarnation: a grasp, that is, of the meaning of Christ's love which led him to suffer and die for man. We need also to know what the meaning of the Church is — of the Church as a "people," of the Church as Christ extended through time and history. But that means we must also ask who Christ is: who he is in relationship to us; who he is in relationship to God the Father to whom he was obedient even unto death; who he is in relationship to the Holy Spirit. And then, too, we need to know how we are to worship God; how we are to believe in him; how we are to serve him. Or take the matter of ethics: What is it to love our neighbor? Does it mean only that we must behave politely toward him, at least until such time as he shows himself opposed to us? Or does it mean we must love him even when he is our enemy? But, if so, what does it mean to love one's enemies? How would such love bear on the relationship between nations? Can a nation behave toward an enemy in the same way in which an individual should?

There are enough problems raised in that paragraph to keep a man or woman busy for a lifetime. In a sense, they are very special problems: one can refuse to confront them, refuse to ask questions, refuse to think about their implications. And of course many people do. They are the kinds of problems and questions which ordinary life can crowd out. Even the laziest people have to give some thought to their food, clothing, and housing; but it requires little effort to evade the larger questions. Our society is well geared to those so inclined; there are innumerable tranquilizers available to ward off anxiety, to keep the larger questions of life and existence from pressing too hard. The Catholic layman will find these tranquilizers readily at hand if he, too, decides that he wants only peace of mind. But he can choose to be different. He can risk thought, risk speculation, risk study, risk the trouble of taking on problems and difficulties, obscurities and mysteries, which will not in the least help him to earn money or impress his friends. And theology is risk: the risk of having old certainties destroyed, of new and perplexing problems raised, of great challenges placed.

Integrity alone calls one to this risk, for it is part of the risk of being a human being, a creature endowed with reason. But the Church also needs laymen who have taken the trouble to think of their place in the

Church and in the world, and who have made an effort to grasp their faith at a deeper level. In the *Constitution on the Church,* promulgated by the Second Vatican Council, the Council fathers said that pastors should assign duties to laymen, "allowing them freedom and room for action. Further, let pastors encourage lay people so that they may undertake tasks on their own initiative. Attentively in Christ, let them consider with fatherly love the projects, suggestions and desires proposed by the laity." Here is an important source of stimulation for the laity. But how will it be answered? By apathy, by indifference, by ignorance, by a laity which has not wrestled with the complexities of setting God's truth in the midst of men? Let us hope not, but little can be expected from the laity unless they know what they are talking about, unless they are capable of venturesome thoughts, generous visions, and perceptive analysis of the Church and the world in which it is situated. Here is a challenge worthy of a man or woman. Here is a reason of the first importance for the laity to take theology seriously.

II

Theology as an Academic Discipline

By F. X. Shea, S. J.

DANIEL CALLAHAN in his introductory chapter to this volume has said that theology will not meet that critical educational test often applied to the most diverse subjects of study by pragmatic students. It will not, as Mr. Callahan points out, make anyone rich. But students are not the only ones who have objections to theology. College professors have their tests, even more educationally critical, and theology seems to fail these too. The professors, or at least large numbers of them, hold that theology will not make anyone smart; that is, that as an academic discipline theology fails to be genuinely intellectual; consequently they, as scholars, want nothing to do with it. For that reason an essay such as this should consider itself to be on the defensive. It is difficult to imagine a similarly titled essay on one of the sciences, e.g., "Biophysics as an Academic Discipline." Why would anyone write such a piece? There is simply no question to be moved. This is not the case with theology. It is a roughly accurate generalization to say that in the academy today theology is not present among the recognized disciplines. A great number of university people are convinced that theology is an illegitimate area of study, at least of that kind of study which they respect as contemporary members of the company of the learned. Consequently theology has been banished from most American universities. Once it was the reigning king (or, more properly, "queen," for intellectual disciplines have, like boats, feminine gender) of the mind's kingdom in the West. Today theology has long since been deposed and figures no more on the university scene than European royal families do on the political.

We will need in this essay to examine the history and present state of theology as a discipline. The history of theology, at least its more remote sections, is sufficiently glorious and there will be the temptation, since my purpose is primarily polemical, to dwell on these. How dare these *parvenus* question such a pedigreed discipline? Could be my stance. But such a procedure would be a mistake. For the charges which have been lodged against theology are being successfully moved and must, as far as possible, be positively dealt with. Alchemy, the precursor of chemistry, had a glorious history too.

In making a defense of theology's claim to true intellectuality I will be concerned to answer the objections of thinkers who are ordinarily called secular, men whose concerns are with the world and time, and who believe that all men should be fully occupied making the quality of life here and now richer, more exciting and fulfilling. These men are often antireligious. I do not believe that there is a necessary connection between what the majority of the secularists positively aim at and the adoption of an antireligious position but, granted the recent history of ideas, it is not surprising to find them in fact antireligious. My argument in defining the nature and limits of theology's academic task will, therefore, throughout most of its length be concerned to refute those whose contempt for theology is radically a contempt for religion. My opponents are the "secular humanists."

"Religion" and Theology

Theology, nevertheless, has other enemies who would seek to bring her down, and whose destructive energies are anything but secular in origin. Religious men of deepest faith and piety have dogged theology throughout her history with fierce denunciation. Indeed, religious objections to the theological enterprise are the most ancient, the most bitter, and the most persistent of all objections; and if the secularist is ever reconciled to theology's work, one can quite confidently predict that on that distant day dedicated religionists will still be viewing it with suspicion.

One can argue that secular opposition is the result of a history of unfortunate and corrigible misunderstanding; religious opposition, on the other hand, seems intrinsic to the discipline. It was there at the beginning of Western theology; it is present today. The author of the Second Epistle of St. Peter seems to have found St. Paul's convoluted thinking about the gospel message a source of possible danger to the faith.[1] I personally recall a very popular Catholic religious leader standing before a mass rally a few years back and announcing over the public address system: "This is the only book," shaking his rosary beads, "the only university that I ever needed." The conviction that hard thought and deep belief are incompatible is common. I hope to demonstrate that these two human and humanizing attitudes are not, in fact, incompatible, that they accompany each man's efforts to embrace reality. They are a fecund duality, opposed indeed but in a polar fashion, as man and woman, not contradictorily, as life and death. Faith vitalizes thought; thought extends faith. Yet the history of theology is a long illustration of how destructive polar oppositions can be. A miasma of suspicion emanates constantly from the faith that quickens thought, and would suppress what it generates. Like the lion of Samson's riddle, religious fidelity can be to theology both savage and sweet.[2]

I have said that the remote academic history of theology in the West is a glorious one, and its glory consists precisely in the fact that it resisted religion in the name of free inquiry. Since I am debating the academic rights of theology primarily with the antireligious secular thinker, it will be pertinent to instance briefly only a few of the more dramatic encounters between theologians insisting on their right to know, and the repressive tendencies of "the simple faithful." But before I do that, let me try to analyze why faith's opposition to theology is so seemingly visceral.

Father Chenu sees it this way:

A Christian, in fact, is convinced of the incompatibility in direct

[1] 2 Pet 3:15–16.
[2] Cf. Jud. 14:14.

proportion to the simplicity of his faith. His loyalty and his trust alike persuade him spontaneously to reject the introduction of rational processes of investigation into this sphere. He is content before the Father in heaven to look upward like a little child, as the Gospels counsel. At his first encounter with Christ he was, indeed, able to demand what were Christ's credentials for making that startling claim to incarnate Godhead; but once he had accepted Christ's love he simply "follows" him. He debates no longer. He harkens. He submits to the testimony of the Holy Spirit.

Many people therefore regard theology — a systematic knowledge, crossbraced by reasons — as a tiresome concession to that spirit of curiosity which is the temptation, gravely misplaced in this instance, lying in wait for Reason. Perhaps I may meet with some "reasons" in the mystery, some proportions and harmonies in the divine encounter, but in so far as I attach myself to such reasons my faith will be imperiled. It will no longer be a pure, simple-hearted attachment to love. Reason, in short, is impertinent — in every sense of the word.[3]

This is an excellent description of the opposition to theology which religious fidelity generates. It is, however, a description of this opposition at its mannerly best. The opposition Father Chenu describes might fruitfully exist within the mind of the theologian himself between his need to accept on the one hand, assert on the other. Augustine knew this tension, and a theological style which cast his dialectic often enough into the form of prayer was one result. Jerome fulminated against the frivolity of worldly learning in the elegantly labored periods he learned from Cicero. Father Chenu's description of religious opposition to theology is eloquent and useful, but it is inadequate to explain how dark and bitter, how really savage, that opposition has frequently become. Theologians are among some of the really great culture heroes of Western history. They are such not merely for the depth and usefulness of their thought, but often enough for the risks — of degradation, of prison, of physical punishment, of death — they ran from the aroused and vengeful indignation of the pious. Such opposition is not sufficiently explained by saying that it finds reason "impertinent" to faith. We must, it seems to me, go into murkier motivations than that.

Pragmatists define knowledge as the search for manipulation and control of the conditions of life. We may legitimately find this too

[3] M. D. Chenu O.P., *Is Theology a Science?* in *The Twentieth Century Encyclopedia of Catholicism*, ed. Henri Daniel-Rops (New York: Hawthorn Books, 1959), p. 13.

narrow a definition, lacking exaltation and sufficient metaphysical penetration. But we can agree with them that knowledge does in fact result in some such control coming into being. About all knowledge there is something Promethean, and the fate of Prometheus awaits all who are so irreverent that they would push on heedlessly, desirous to know, and thus to expose to human will and control, the secrets of the gods. Such men, so the religious-minded of all ages have instinctively believed, must feel the thunderbolt.

One can agree perhaps with many of our contemporary secular intellectuals that a rough correlation can probably be established between the cultural grip of a religious faith and the social and technical retrogression of a given people. Where religion is strong, knowledge is retarded. One has only to survey the history of Egypt, of Mesopotamia, of the great Eastern cultures, of what can be known of the Inca, Aztec, and Mayan civilizations, or view the social structures of Tibet, to recognize that religion does in fact often inhibit intellectual exploration. Each of these histories follows the same pattern: progress to a certain point (the progress usually accompanied by vigorous religious questioning, i.e., theology), then a fear of stirring the wrath of supernal powers succeeding to strangle off or at least check further progress. Often too the theocratic civilizations found that they could not learn from each other, even when their ritual prohibitions did not so restrict contact that they could not know one another's accomplishments and skills, because what it was permitted to learn in one society might well be religiously taboo in the next. The remarkable history of the Western complex of peoples and its ability to learn and transfer its learning from one religious context to another might be variously explained. But we may be forgiven if we suggest that its inception can be usefully dated from the day Plato equipped the inquiring mind with a commission for courage by writing the sentence about the unexamined life's being not worth living. Plato's master, of course, died for impiety.

This pattern of things — religious awe, envy, and resentment of the Protheans — is not something we have need to exemplify with instances from the remote past. Any barbershop on a busy day can offer two or three amateur Torquemadas deploring "those scientists" and all their works and pomps. ("If God intended us to be on the moon, He'd have put us there.") And during these last few centuries of technological acceleration, those Western countries which have been conspicuously slothful have been precisely those where religion has remained a powerful social and political force. It is perhaps salutary to point out in this essay intended for a Catholic textbook, that, scandalously enough, these countries have been just those where Catholicism has exercised a nearly theocratic role — the European countries of the Mediterranean and those of South America. It is a roughly accurate generalization to say, further, that those countries such as Ghana, where Christian missionaries were a relatively minor force during the period of colonial domination, have proved better prepared in education, in civil service, in political sophistication, for independence than countries such as the Congo, where the missionary was a pervasive presence.

I am aware that such observations are used frequently by the secularist to support his rejection of theology. But, this is an error which arises from a failure to distinguish between religion and theology. While I might agree, with nothing of the delight of the secularist, that "where religion is strong, knowledge is retarded" this is, nevertheless, not true of theology. There are decent enough arguments against the academic legitimacy of theology, but this is not one of them. For the objections of religious commitment to the scientific enterprise fall first and heaviest on theology itself. The first Prometheans were the theologians. Perhaps they are still the most courageous.

Reed experimenting with yellow fever in his jungle hospital, Fermi drawing the rods out of an atomic pile under the Chicago Stadium, the astronaut supine in his contour chair waiting out the countdown — these are justly admired explorers of the unknown. But the terrors of the unknown they seek to penetrate do not encompass eternity. The offense of their errors can only be offered to a limited power. The theologian by the premises of his own faith questions God, challenges, perhaps in ways whose irreverence he will never know, an omnipotence. If this all seems a touch dramatically strained, it is nothing but the sober truth for the theologian himself who must, of course, be a believer to be a theologian at all; and even if he had not to worry about internal doubt, there were always for the theologian the external dangers which the overbold thinker about matters religious had to face and which offered verifiable evidence of the dangers of his trade.

St. Athanasius, bishop of Alexandria, was forcibly deposed by his Arian enemies five times and lived his life in fear of physical harm. Arius, the heresiarch (but one whose honesty there is no warrant for doubting at this distance) and Athanasius' opponent, supposedly died of poison. The medieval insistence on the rights of the mind to think critically about the truths of faith created the turbulent times of change and counterchange in which the Western university first achieved its power and independent existence. To quote Richard Hofstadter: "The role of those whose ideas received some measure of unfavorable attention from some ecclesiastical authority from the twelfth to the four-teenth century is impressive — Roscellinus, Abelard, Gilbert de la Porree, Roger Bacon, Siger de Brabant, Peter John Olivi, Annald of Villanova, Meister Eckhart, William of Ockham, Nicholas of Autrecourt, Pietro d' Abano, Marsillus of Padua — even Peter Lombard and Aquinas."[4] It should be remembered that, while it has been customary to exaggerate the authoritarian horrors of life in the medieval establishment where the space for free inquiry was by no means as narrow as it has often been pictured, nevertheless "some measure of unfavorable attention from ecclesiastical authorities" was not a small threat to men whose liveli-hood, if only occasionally their physical well-being, depended rather immediately upon the favor of ecclesiastical authorities.

I have already stated that I have no intention of recounting at any length the contributions which theology made to the widening of the hu-man horizons during the days of its flourishing. History is neither the aim nor the method of this essay. I simply wish here at the beginning to recall that theology's contributions to human knowledge have not been small, nor were they easily achieved. No discipline, I think it can be said, has had as tempestuous a course. For every Galileo persecuted with imprisonment, theology can cite a number actually killed. For every Madame Curie struck down by the secret power of the thing she investigated, theology has perhaps hundreds burdened with the doubts and lonely fears of men who would bring their Maker to judgment. The great period of theology was the Middle Ages, and even a cursory review of those times is sufficient to vindicate the adjective Promethean for theology: Abelard, the sacramental contro-versies, the establishment of Aristotle, the nominalist dispute, the critiques of papal power and those of mendicant orders, concilarism, and finally the sixteenth century in which men filled with the theological spirit of courage and fidelity died like flies for their opinions on all sides of a divided Christendom.

Yet despite its past, theology is without position, "class," in the intellec-tual hierarchy today. That at the minimum is a fair statement of its

---

[4] Richard Hofstadter and Walter P. Metzger, *The Development of Academic Free-dom in the United States* (New York: Columbia University Press, 1955), p. 15.

situation. Not entirely out of currency (my previous aside which implied a comparison with alchemy was to overstate the case), it does not enjoy much regard from the intellectual world of which the university can be taken as the central forum. We must see the title of this essay as a question: Is theology an academic discipline? And to answer it we will need to take up with some order and seriousness the many objections to its achieving place and "class" again.

THE ECLIPSE OF THEOLOGY

Prior to the Reformation, while theologians continued to run risks by insisting on their right to bring intellectual clarity to the measure of the possible into religious materials, a new group of thinkers and scholars began to emerge who also, indeed in their day, perhaps more so, deserved the title Prometheans. These were, first, the humanists, and then the experimentalists. With the familiar, tragic irony of human event, their prosecutors were often theologians. Richard Hofstadter's history of academic freedom is very instructive on this point. For about forty pages his heroes of freedom are religious thinkers; for the next two hundred and thirty odd pages such men are the villains.[5]

The sins of theologians against free inquiry begin with the emergence of humanistic learning. Hofstadter's interest is, like mine, one in the academic, that is in the university, situation. Therefore his remark about the development of universities at the time that the theologians turned reactionary and repressive is, I think, pertinent: "As universities became more heavily endowed with college foundations and other properties, and as their intellectual life became increasingly committed to permanent libraries, they became timid and immobile, and their financial dependence provided princes and muncipalities with a pretext for unprecedented intervention in their affairs."[6] In other words, the theologians could not be as free to criticize and were often more interested in protecting their own position than in furthering their own search for truth. Humanism was able to make its first encroachments on the intellectual scene because for the most part it grew outside the university under a system of private patronage (as in some measure

---

[5] *Ibid.* The work is divided into two parts. Hofstadter deals with the first, a 274 page treatment of the earlier period in American Higher Education entitled "The Age of the College." The first chapter of Hofstadter's section, "The European Heritage" has proved most useful for the present study.

[6] *Ibid.*, p. 41.

did the experimental sciences afterward).[7] But by the time the linguistic skills and disciplines which the humanists developed were mature enough to request legitimate place in the university, humanism found the scholastic theologians had set their faces against it. It "was a threat to academic vested interests."[8]

I would like, for the sake of the case I have to make, to be able to pursue this line. For it can be insinuated that theology's present low position in the university has no other reason but its injudicious use of academic power in its halcyon days, implying, of course, that vengefulness, not conviction, is all that really prevents its receiving serious academic consideration today. I think an interesting case could be made. It would not, however, be conclusive. There is more at work in the present disregard of theology's academic contributions than can be explained by the *Realpolitik* of scholarship. In order to make their way against an enthroned and tyrannical scholastic theology, humanism, and science — and the philosophies and intellectual systems attendant on these two movements — created over the course of two centuries a criticism of theology which went very deep — to the bone. There is no present possibility of theology's recovering academic status unless it is prepared to take serious note of the critical analysis its aims and methods have been subjected to.

The Humanists' Objections To Theology

The humanists were professionally skeptical of analysis. They protested vigorously the endless analytic refinements of the schoolmen. Paradoxically this protest was often motivated by a desired return to precisely that simple religious fidelity against which theology during the twelfth-century revival of learning had to make its way. Erasmus and Thomas More protested the pretentiousness, the rationalistic industry of the schoolmen in terms very reminiscent of St. Bernard's handwringing over Abelard. It was irreverent, contentious, and worked to the detriment of piety.[9] By the time Hobbes came to write *Leviathan*,

---

[7] The most influential center of humanism was the Platonic Academy of Florence under the conduct of Marsileus of Ficino. Kristeller attributes its success directly to the relative weakness of the University of Florence. Cf. Paul Oskar Kristeller, *Renaissance Thought II*, Chapter IV, "The Platonic Academy of Florence" (New York: Harper Torchbooks, 1965), p. 89 ff.

[8] Hofstadter and Metzger, *op. cit.*, p. 48.

[9] I offer this as a one sentence summary of, say, Erasmus' *Praise of Folly* which never tires of thumping the theologians on precisely these points. Cf. *inter alia:* "And devoutly, no doubt, did the apostles consecrate the Eucharist; yet, had they

he had behind him a century of humanistic jibes and philological criticism to support his heavy-handed mockery of scholastic terms.[10] By the end of the seventeenth century, the technical philosophical language of the medieval theologians was no longer a shared instrument of communication throughout scholarly Europe. It probably will never be again; and one is justified in regretting this. Mathematics has developed as the *lingua franca* of the learned; and happy as the results of this development have been, no one will deny that there are many concerns of great importance to the mind which will never find mathematics a fit instrument for their expression. The attempt to revive scholastic language and dialectical method which one finds frequently enough, particularly among Catholic philosophers and theologians, is a quixotic effort no doubt, but understandable.

Not much has to be said at this point in history in answer to the humanist's objections to theology. There never was much theoretic point to their criticism. The attack they mounted against the language of the schools was, as we have just said, highly successful, but not remarkably intelligent. The humanists were fastidious philologists and their refined ears were offended by medieval barbarisms. Yet the language of the schools had been created to serve honest purposes by men wrestling with real problems in a rigorously precise way. New barbarisms, after the humanists destroyed the old have been, as they had to be, invented — the linguistic contortions of the social sciences have been too often parodied to need further mockery from me — and the only difference the humanistic fastidiousness has succeeded in creating is that we have a great deal more difficulty in understanding our intellectual past or even one another today, than we would possibly have had, had the language of learned men been allowed to continue without destruction. The criticism which the humanists made in the name of religious piety of the intellectual pretensions of theology is not one which anyone devoted to the mind can take seriously. Perhaps the humanists themselves did not take it seriously except as a

---

been asked the question touching the 'terminus a quo' and the 'terminus ad quem' of transubstantiation; of the manner how the same body can be in several places at one and the same time; of the difference the body of Christ has in heaven from that of the cross, or this in the Sacrament; in what point of time transubstantiation is, whereas prayer, by means of which it is, as being a discrete quantity, is transient; they would not, I conceive, have answered with the same subtlety as the Scotists dispute and define it." Ann Arbor Paperbacks edition of John Wilson's translation, p. 94.

[10] Cf. esp. *Leviathan* Part I, ch. 5.

more or less successful weapon against a powerful and entrenched enemy.

Yet, despite the intellectual poverty of the humanists' attack on theology as it was practiced in the sixteenth century, the attack was successful. The humanists made an historically important contribution to the present low academic estate of theology. They were able to do this because sixteenth-century theologians, unknown to themselves, cooperated handsomely in their own undoing. Theology by the sixteenth century had become tyrannical. By ignoring humanistic interest in philological knowledge, by refusing to listen when the linguistic scholars offered criticisms of traditional theological readings of classical and biblical texts, theology did much more than merely make life hard for good and harmless men — it refused to be informed. Tyranny in matters of the mind is evil because of what it does to others; it is stupid, however, because of what it does to itself. A tyrant soon becomes isolated and an isolated discipline soon becomes irrelevant.

One of the most successful canards in the intellectual folklore of the West must be the assertion that the schoolmen used to discuss the number of angels which could dance on the head of a pin. It was doubtless a witticism of some anonymous seventeenth-century humanist; it remains a commonplace of the twentieth-century intellectual. In fact no record can be found that any question even in the vicinity of that for silliness was the proposition of actual scholastic dispute; but the irrelevance of late medieval theological study to the real interests and real problems of the times was no canard.[11] Irrelevancy which made it vulnerable to attack, tyranny which made attack a certainty, these were the characteristics of sixteenth-, seventeenth-, eighteenth-century theology; and they were, as is evident, highly injurious characteristics. Wherever theology was strong, it was censorious, exclusive, obtuse. It had little to say pertinent to a civilization which was rapidly changing, and it seemed incapable of learning to speak pertinently. The humanists' charges remained effectively true, and contributed well in excess of their intrinsic worth to the waning of theology's *eclat*.

The position of theology within the domestic purlieus of an American Catholic campus is not so dissimilar to that held by the Renaissance

---

[11] After this passage was set in print, a man learned in such matters pointed out to me that Thomas Aquinas (at a place he was unable to recall) used angels dancing on the head of a pin as an illustration of pointless subject for scholastic dispute. If his recollection is accurate, and I assume it to be, I am clearly wrong in assigning the invention of this piece of nonsense to the seventeenth century. But as Thomas' intention seems to have been essentially the same as mine, I think I am justified in letting the rest of my observation stand as written.

schoolmen that a pause here to underline some possible lessons from that time would be entirely out of place. Theology is strongly entrenched in the curriculum. Unlike the situation in the nonsectarian American university, theology in the Catholic university has a place and what power a large department can generate on relatively small campuses. Often its power is employed to restrict discussion, particularly of those issues which it feels fall especially under its competence. Instances are not unknown, even in those enlightened, post-Johannine days, of theology departments effecting the dismissal of teachers of disturbing opinions even from other university departments. Such actions, where they are not in fact taken, are sometimes threatened, and are quite widely feared. Furthermore, theology is rather constantly under attack. The Catholic university is not sealed off from the rest of the world. The disregard of theology on the intellectual scene at large is well known both to students and professors. Its power is resentfully conceded and grudgingly borne. The campus newspaper is commonly full of attacks on the privileges of theology. These, no more than the attacks of the humanists, are ordinarily undistinguished for their critical solidity; but they can glitter here and there with a mica of wit. The situation is disturbingly parallel to that in the sixteenth century. However there is one heartening aspect: if it is true that one can learn from the past, the course theology should take on the Catholic campus is clear.

It must above all learn humility. It must learn to listen even where the opinion proposed seems flatly to contradict orthodoxy. A reconciliation between the novel and the traditional is the very pattern of learning — something that only the moribund mind does not admit. Theology, like any discipline, if it is to grow and expand, must change ceaselessly. Second, theology, if it is to survive on the Catholic campus, must insist on becoming and remaining relevant. For example, the doctrine of Christ is often taught as though it were especially designed to smite Arius and Nestorius hip and thigh. Clearly, in any nuanced understanding of the Church's faith in Christ, a treatment of the Christological controversies will find place. But it is not unthinkable that a full and rewarding undergraduate course could be taught without the precision which a study of the early councils would bring to the question entering in as one of the course objectives, or even being present at all (except, presumably, in the instructor's own understanding of the material). A course on the doctrine of Christ might legitimately be more interested in the relevancy of, say, an existentialist or Freudian view of human nature to the Incarnation, or in a Teilhardist extension of the Pauline cosmological texts. It might never once deal with the Arian problem; and yet speak to students both more intellectually and stimulatingly than any number of more exhaustive reviews of the doctrine. Above all today theology must seek to speak both to, and out of, the actual faith of today's students or it has reason to fear that even its privileged position on the Catholic campus will not be proof against the kind of forces which brought down the schoolmen.

THEOLOGY AND THE NEW SCIENCE

The attacks of the humanists were directed at the subject matter with which the theology of the late Middle Age and of the early Renaissance schoolmen occupied its time. The lasting lesson of that period is that theology, the same as any other discipline, cannot be healthy if it ignores the real questions of the age for those which, while they might have great historical significance, are in contemporary terms nugatory. But as a matter of fact some of the questions which agitated the scholastics' disputations at the time proved to be of immense importance for the future of human knowledge. Ironically it was these questions precisely which stimulated the scorn and satire of the humanists more than any others. For the late scholastics were very profoundly concerned with problems connected with the motion of physical bodies. Herbert Butterfield traces the sources of modern science to the problems which some Aristotelian thinkers at Merton College, Oxford were having in reconciling the Aristotelian theory of motion with the observed actions of an arrow in flight.[12] The humanists mocking the schoolmen were, in some respects, quarreling not so much with the proponents of a worn-out theology as with the precursors of modern science.

It is often assumed that religion and science are in some sort of inevitable tension. And indeed they are, but we are allowed to say that only if we include theology among the sciences. Knowledge and devotion are true opposites, polar opposites as we have seen, between which there can exist a field of force either productive or destructive as the actual will, of historical personages decide. Between the knowledge derived from Aristotle and a profound religious commitment, there was

[12] Herbert Butterfield, *The Origins of Modern Science* (New York: Macmillan, paperback edition, 1960), p. 10 ff.

harmony in the mind and writing of Thomas Aquinas. Between the knowledge derived from Copernicus and the religious commitment of many of his contemporaries if not himself, there was excited disharmony in the case of Galileo. The tension is always there, producing various results. But, between sciences as such there is no inevitable tension. A chemist and a theologian may very greatly disagree and the reasons for their quarrel may be good or frivolous, personal or objective, but these reasons cannot legitimately be reduced to the fact that one of the disputants is a chemist, the other a theologian. Both are scientists; both are bound by their professions to use evidence for their arguments. Yet it is clear that according to contemporary use of the word, "scientist" is employed equivocally of a theologian and chemist. The theologian has no laboratory. He offers no propositions which can be validated under controlled conditions in such a way that everyone can come to the identical conclusions. He is not, then, in the ordinary modern sense a scientist. Now the word "science," as we know, at its root, simply means "knowledge." One might conclude that since a theologian (or a philosopher or literary critic) is no longer called a scientist or "knower" then an active effort was made at some point in history to restrict the scope of the word "science" to those knowers who knew in the manner of physical experimenters. This, of course, is true.

The disciplines we now distinguish from others by the name, physical sciences, have been accompanied throughout their relatively short history by an attendant swarm of celebrators. Sometimes we like to think that we are blasé about science. At least those of us who have listened sympathetically to the criticisms of science made by modern humanists, especially since about 1800, would prefer to remain detached from excessive popular enthusiasm. A student of literature can smile over Bacon's expectations in *The New Atlantis* that refrigeration and plumbing would bring a kind of salvation to mankind. Yet let some dramatic breakthrough take place in physical technology or theory — space exploration offers a handy instance — and he is a world-weary esthete indeed who can ignore the excitement.

Excitement has been the characteristic atmosphere in which the sciences have worked since they first emerged in the seventeenth century. As intellectual historians push the origins of science further and further back into the Middle Ages, even to the ancients, they do not change the fact that the scientists of the seventeenth century had a sense of creating something fundamentally new; and that sense, that a radical departure for the human spirit was achieved by the physical sciences, has accompanied their progress ever since. In some ways this has been fostered more by their retinue than by the scientists themselves. Philosophers of science have often been concerned to make clear to the rest of the world what a marvelous novelty the sciences have been. It is not, I think, insignificant that most of the philosophers of science have not been themselves distinguished scientists. Like hero-worshiping boys, they are honored to carry the stars' uniforms. Particularly today the philosophers of science who are themselves scientists of note — one thinks of Whitehead, Schrödinger and Bronowski — are concerned to demonstrate affinities between the operations of the scientific mind and those of minds engaged in different areas. But nevertheless a conviction that "science" is different from, and superior to, other kinds of knowledge has persisted more or less strongly since the late renaissance and has profoundly affected the academic scene, with most serious consequences for the regard accorded theology.

What is this new and different note which the physical sciences are thought to have introduced into human knowledge? Bacon considered it to be the empirical method. But the empirical method was not unknown to the men of ancient times and the Middle Ages. Not only in those propaedeutics to modern science, astrology, and alchemy, or in the rudimentary science that was ancient medicine and physics, but even in metaphysics and theology some use of empirical evidence was known and valued. Illustrations were constantly used for all general principles and may be taken as pointing the way to rigorous empiric proof. Even theological propositions were felt to be stronger if they could be supported by evidence which appealed to the senses. This is probably the explanation for the proliferation of miracle stories. Bleeding hosts were a kind of positive evidence for transubstantiation. Positivism, that preference for evidence which can be seen and handled, is not in itself inimical either to theology or "nonscientific" thinking of any kind. The senses, so immediately and finally persuasive, are frequently the last discriminators, as they are the first instigators, of knowledge. The men of the seventeenth century did not discover this. What they did discover was a way of accumulating and ordering sense evidence "scientifically," which is to say in a way that yielded a large harvest of assured knowledge.

Bacon could call his description of the inductive, empirical method of investigation the *Novum Organum* because he expected, quite rightly as it turned out, that a contribution to human knowledge and control of nature would result from it is at least the equal of that achieved by Aristotle's book on deductive logic, *The Organum*. However, one can doubt that Bacon really understood the actual achievement of Galileo and Harvey and the others whose methods he was attempting to analyze. There was some confusion in his mind and in the minds of many in that explosive century, when so much was so new, between the two attacks on the scholastic method. The humanists, as we saw, rightly objected to irrelevance in theology, but wrongly to its elaborate and clumsy language of precision. Many of the advocates of the "new science" since they also had objections against scholasticism, adopted the language of the humanists. The impression became current that the sins of the scholastics consisted in being too abstract and that the new science's advantage was that it was concrete because it had developed a highly successful way of employing empirical proof in the interests of knowledge. Yet, at this distance at least, it seems very clear that the really distinct contribution of the scientific method as it came into use in the seventeenth century was just the opposite to such reading of their history. What science newly offered was a brilliant way to achieve a greater degree of abstraction in dealing with natural phenomena than had been possible before.

> ". . .we do not in real life have perfectly spherical balls moving on perfectly horizontal planes — the trick lay in the fact that it occurred to Galileo to imagine these. Furthermore, even when men were coming extraordinarily near to what we would call the truth about local motion, they did not clinch the matter — the thing did not come out clear and clean — until they had realized and had made completely conscious to themselves the fact that they were in reality transposing the question into a different realm. They were discussing not real bodies as we actually observe them in the real world, but geometrical bodies moving in a world without resistence and without gravity — moving in that boundless emptiness of Euclidean space which Aristotle had regarded as unthinkable . . .[13]

To put the matter another way: it has been customary, since Bacon and Locke, and until very recently when the revision of Newtonian cosmology created by the men of our own century forced a rethinking of the question, to consider that the distinctive mark of the scientific method was the experiment; and that what was distinctive about the

---

[13] *Ibid.*, p. 5.

experiment was that it rooted knowledge in the concrete, three-dimensional world which is available to everyone. Now it becomes clearer every day that what was distinctive about the new knowledge was not so much the experiment but what went before the experiment (the hypothesis), what accompanied the experiment (the control), and what followed the experiment (the generalization); and in each case these elements were marked by an extraordinary, judged by earlier norms, degree of abstraction.

It is not because the scientist is more "realistic" that he is successful. Rather it is because the scientist is willing to abandon the world as he knows it for a conceptually modeled world of fantastic simplicity – one or two bodies rather than teeming abundance of concrete nature – that he is able to design experiments where only a few factors are allowed to operate, the rest being controlled out of consideration. It is his readiness to abstract from the actual conditions of experience which makes him able to obtain such firm results and win for these results such wide acceptance. The language of his abstract thought is the empty language of the visual symbol, of mathematics, where the semantic units have been allowed by careful elimination to have no history and consequently no penumbra of emotion. Far more important for scientific success than the experiment was the development of that mathematical manner of thought which received such marked emphasis during the seventeenth century and which made the pointed and pragmatically limited experiment possible.

Since this manner of viewing the methods of science contradicts popularizations of long standing, many of which are still current in unimpeachably intellectual circles, I should like, even at the risk of annoying those who have long since caught the point, to belabor it. The epistemological status of the word "fact" is a murky one – but it seems to name, in most contexts, an object whose ontological reality is discernable by the senses. That at any rate seems to be the intention of most speakers who use "fact" as the distinguishing mark of scientific knowledge: "Science deals with facts," is an example of the kind of context I mean. In such a statement nonscientific ways of knowing are seen by implication to deal with the nonfactual. The assertive existentiality of "the fact" is what is operating in such a sentence, so spoken; and the aim is to credit science with being the only legitimate approach to the ontological – all else is nonreal. Ontological reality and its discernability by sense perception, the two characteristics of "the fact" as we defined it, strongly reinforce each other in this view. Indeed sense perception, at least when rationally controlled so that it becomes the basis for invariant experiment, is often, for the people whose opinions we are presently concerned to understand, the single secure footing for knowledge of the real.[14]

One finds this view to be behind Hume's famous conclusion to *The Enquiry concerning Human Understanding*, that no time can be profitably spent studying any proposition which does not contain either the report of an experiment or a mathematical argument.[15] The factual view of science informs the epistemological theories of Russell and many of the logical positivistic school of our own times. It recommends itself by being hardheaded, humble, and properly suspicious of high-flying concepts. Given enough time and industry, it would assert, the whole of reality can be pieced out and woven together by the co-operative industry of scientific investigators. Leaving aside for the moment the difficult question of whether a sensible test is the final arbiter of truth, one can reject this narrow epistemology on two counts: (1) its minimalism, seemingly so modest, actually rejects with serene arrogance not only most of the thinking about knowledge which has come down to us, but even the greater amount of knowledge theory current in our own day; (2) it seems fairly certain that, as an analysis of the actual method of the scientists it celebrates, it is mistaken.

Scientists as a matter of fact do not devise experiments to establish facts; they devise experiments to test and validate theories. The theories come first and these are conceptual, the result of insight into experience. In a psychological sense the genesis of insight may well be as subjective and incommunicable as a love affair. Boyle's theory of gases may well have owed as much to his religious scruples as to his tinkering

[14] Sometime, on the other hand, the sensibility of "the fact" is paramount in the speaker's intention and often this is accompanied by a purpose of disparaging science. Science is a humdrum, utilitarian work of the mind, dealing with what is readily available to *mere* sense perception. Sense perception, for those who hold such opinions, misses those heights and profundities which are proper to human knowledge. Such a significance to "factual science" is often intended by those who would defend theology against its detractors. Let me only say that I think this is a most unfortunate stand from which to mount theology's defense. Theology, like any discipline, must use the senses, like any discipline it has its patches of dull work and is not forever flying off to peaks of exultation or mucking about in subliminal depths of despair.

[15] Cf. David Hume, *Enquiries*, ed. L. A. Selby-Bigge, Oxford University Press, p. 165.

with the air pump. Such an example is perhaps excessively controversial since it is a deliberate flouting of accepted attitudes. But would one say that Freud's psychological constructs, his model of unconscious desire, is entirely the result of a neutral survey of "the facts"? No, the pattern of insight is fairly clear even if the etiology of any given insight is probably unavailable even to the thinker who experiences it.

The positivists are weakest when they propose the neutrally perceived fact as the source for ideas or insight. Positivism is rather shaky as a noetic theory. What its advocates actually seem to be expressing is a desire: perceived fact *ought* to be the origin of ideas because, as four centuries of science have demonstrated, unless ideas can be validated by empirical test they should be regarded with the gravest suspicion. Indeed, even after such validation, they should be warily adopted. Here positivism is on very firm ground indeed. No lesson has been more successfully enforced by the intellectual experience of the age of science, than that all concepts can be forged into fetters for the mind. The widespread use of the controlled experiment has been, time and time again, the liberator of understanding from the tyranny of accepted conceptual frameworks. A test, designed to support a theory, gives unexpected results and concludes in the theory's destruction. (The Michelson-Morley experiment which set out to establish the existence of the ether is a case in point.) Nevertheless the experiment's design is the outcome of a framework, and it is simply not possible to determine to what degree the design has prejudiced the results.

For centuries the Aristotelians of Greece, the Arab world, and Europe had, in the rising of fire and the falling of rain, empirical verification of the proposition that "each thing seeks its natural place." This was not faulty thinking on their part; to insist that it was is to read history backwards. In our own day the contradiction in current theories of the nature of light is elegantly supported by empirical evidence. (I presume that any man of sense will give no houseroom to those anarchistic noetics which would admit the possibility of flat contradictions existing in reality.) Either side of the wave-particle contradiction can be supported. If we design a test to ask a wave question, we get a wave answer. Put the question in such a form that the experiment seeks to verify the particle hypothesis, and the results marvelously support particles. For all experimental tests are questions asked by particular questioners and like the cross-examining lawyer the questioner has an answer in mind.

In all of this I am not seeking to destroy confidence in the methods of science. To attempt to do so would be foolish. Science is impervious to such dog-in-the-manger polemics. What I am attempting to do is to make clear what are the actual differences between the procedures of the scientist and the theologian. For too long it has been assumed that the scientist works empirically, factually, inductively; the theologian was presumed to operate in an almost diametrically opposite way; abstractly, dogmatically, deductively. What I want to establish is that, put this way, the description of the differing methods is just not true of either. With James B. Conant I am convinced that the search for a special method and, consequently, for a special critical philosophy which will belong exclusively to the physical science is bootless.

> There is no such thing as *the* scientific method. If there were, surely an examination of the history of physics, chemistry, and biology would reveal it. For as I have already pointed out, few would deny that it is the progress in physics, chemistry, and experimental biology which gives everyone confidence in the procedures of a scientist. Yet, a careful examination of these subjects fails to reveal any *one* method by means of which masters in these fields broke new ground.[16]

It is the progress, the results, the successes of the sciences which have created a universal trust in these disciplines of the mind, not a special form of procedure which they invented and patented. When theology was succesful, when it built the great universities and first established the international community of scholars who could defy, if need be, baron and bishop, when it imposed its then current view of a hierarchically ordered universe as *the* social model on an unruly populace, when it inspired chivalry and monasticism, then *its* procedures and methods were unquestioned. All disciplines on close examination at least work methodologically pretty much the same way. The same tools of investigation are available to all. A discipline is more usefully distinguished by its area of study than by its methods, though in saying this I am not denying that disciplines are also differentiated by the frequency or intensity with which they favor one or another moment in the noetic process.

The success of experimental science, over against theology, seemed to the men of the seventeenth century to arise from its willingness to validate its theories empirically, to submit theory to fact. This

[16] Cf. *Science and Common Sense* (New Haven and London: Yale Paperbound, 1951), p. 45.

was a factor in their success certainly, but it followed upon a more important methodological decision which was often overlooked both then and since, namely, the decision to ignore all elements of a problem which could not be worked into a predetermined conceptual design. The theory, not its test, was the really significant thing. Thus the sciences were able to achieve a specialization of intellectual concern which brought problems into very sharp focus and suggested empirical verification, but they did this by limiting the area of inquiry and by employing abstraction to a degree previously unheard of.

THEOLOGY AND ABSTRACTION

Renaissance humanists objected to the then reigning theology because it concerned itself with the wrong questions. Theology had become so addicted to abstraction, Aristotelian logic and metaphysics, that its work offered nothing to religious devotion. And that, as the humanists saw it, was theology's ultimate purpose: to utter, while it criticized, belief and worship. Renaissance scientists, on the other hand, had no objections to the religious irrelevance of the questions which the theologians were moving concerning the motions of heavens and the order of causes; what they found objectionable was that the theologians, because they refused to abstract sufficiently from the actual conditions of observation, were moving the questions in the wrong way. During the Renaissance then, theology was objected to on two counts: it was too abstract, and it was too concrete.

Since the objections to theology's academic legitimacy which we have seen arising from the new science are objections to its methods rather than its subject matter, perhaps it is time we initiated a discussion of the methods of theology. There will be more of this later. First of all, theology *is* a science in the older sense of that word. It seeks to create knowledge which is systematic and reasoned out of evidence. It has promethean aspirations and its drive to own and possess true knowledge — which is to say, to undergo the experience of certainty — brings down on its head the objections of the religiously minded. It is theology's willingness, however, to limit its promethean desires, the degree to which it is content with uncertainty, that is at the heart of all the many varieties of scientific objections to its continued existence. Certain knowledge is not of the same crucial importance to theology as it is to science, nor can theology ever let certainty become so important without losing its own essential character.

For the sake of certainty, science, by which word here I mean the drive and will to know in the security that what is known is known without shadow of doubt, will sacrifice anything. If no certainty can be obtained in some areas, the true scientist will ignore these even though they may be of more intrinsic interest to him as a person, as a man, than the areas he chooses to investigate. Thus the interrelationships of men in a large metropolis are doubtless of greater intrinsic interest than the social structures of an ant heap. But the total scientist, driven by his passion to know purely and without shadow of doubt, will abandon the investigation of the first for the second because, being more observable, more manipulable, the ant heap can be "checked out" to a point much nearer exhaustive knowledge than the denser, more complicated city of men. It may well be that in doing this the total scientist will find patterns of ant behavior which are useful for understanding the actions of metropolitan men. In fact this often has been the result. The sciolists of Swift's Laputa in the third voyage of *Gulliver's Travels* were as absurd as Swift's massive talent for portraying the absurd could paint them. Yet all or nearly all of their trivial or obscene projects have been pursued in some scientific context or other and have wonderfully assisted men to create that impressive measure of control over our material environment which we enjoy in the twentieth century.[17]

The most essential characteristic of a true scientist is the readiness with which he will value the pattern of things beyond their substance. We have seen how the real advantage Renaissance science enjoyed over scholastic Aristotelianism was its readiness to mathematize, to conceive a pure, abstract state of intelligibility that loftily prescinded from the limiting conditions of concrete reality. It is well to remember that the presiding intellect over the birth of Renaissance science, as it was for humanism, was Plato for whom the materiality of things was the sole obstacle to knowledge. Schrödinger, explaining the subatomic world, assures us that Plato is still the scientific master today, when he asserts that "Form, not substance is the fundamental concept."[18]

Pure science, then, has a passion for certainty; it sees certainty based securely only on order, form, the repeatable pattern beneath the unique

---

[17] Swift probably thought his scatological imagination had reached the outer bounds of absurdity when he had his Laputians carefully weighing stools; but this is a procedure much in favor with behavioristic researchers today.

[18] Erwin Schrödinger, *Science and Humanism* (Cambridge: Cambridge University Press, 1952). The sentence quoted is the title of the fourth chapter of this illuminating essay, cf. p. 18 ff.

moments of time and human events. To find and asseverate that pattern it will risk anything. The forest is never to be missed, even where there may happen to be no trees. Theology knows this passion for certainty and the loveliness of the shapes that certainty feeds on; but theology cannot risk everything in order to know and remain theology. There is a limit to its right to abstract which it must always acknowledge. In the same sense that poetry is a less pure art than music, that medicine a less pure science than biology, that physics is less pure than mathematics, theology is less purely scientific than the sciences which flourished out of its academic defeat.

The limiting condition which checks the scientific impulse in the theologian is faith. The theologian cannot abandon faith, any more than the geologist can abandon the earth. Faith is the object of his inquiry, the manifold reality he seeks to reduce to order. If he prefers the ordering principles and patterns he discovers in his inquiries to the substance of the faith, he may well initiate a new, even valuable area of knowledge, but he is no longer rightly called a theologian. Thus theology is often the first academic love of people who eventually become biblical critics or archeologists or students of comparative religion. For there are now a whole host of ancillary disciplines which surround the theologian's main concern.

> "Philosophy," wrote Galileo, "is written in that vast book which stands ever open before our eyes, I mean the universe: but it cannot be read until we have learned the language and become familiar with the characters in which it is written. It is written in mathematical language, and the letters are triangles, circles and other geometrical figures, without which means it is humanly impossible to comprehend a single word."[19]

Galileo was brilliantly correct about everything, but his main proposition — namely, to ignore all qualitative considerations in nature, was not philosophy. It was something new and Renaissance philosophy could not follow him in his passion for quantitative patterns without losing its own identity. Much less so, could theology.

Faith is ordinarily taken by those who see little human value to theological study as the theologian's secret disgrace, the idiot child to be kept hidden in the attic. Because theology accepts faith as central to its enterprise it cannot be "objective" knowledge. It cannot, as they see

---

[19] Cited from E. A. Burtt, *The Metaphysical Foundations of Modern Science* (New York: Doubleday Anchor Books, 1954), p. 75.

it, contribute genuinely to man's knowledge of himself and his world. The least a decently academic man can do who is also a theologian is to experience shame at this aspect of his profession.

There are, of course, answers at least to the presuppositions of this line of objection which I will deal with later on. Let it be enough here to say that theology's refusal to abstract beyond the point permitted it by its commitment to faith could well prove its strength. Whether this is true or not, our purpose at the moment is merely to point out that theological science *had* to refuse the solicitations of the Renaissance scientists to mathematicize because if it had not, it would have become, as it did nearly become in fact in the Cambridge Platonists, the Cartesian and Leibnizian theologians, *e.g.*, Malebranche, Spinoza *et al.*, a sterile rationalism, a "science of faith" in which the scientific intention had so dominated that little of faith could any longer be discerned. While one or another thinker may, for reasons which persuade him, decide that theology is no true discipline of the mind, and politely ask it, therefore, to go away, he cannot rightfully ask it to become something other than it is. The solicitations made to theology to follow the lead of the new sciences into a world of mental patterns would have made theology the science of something else — metaphysics, theodicy — not any longer the science of faith.

Faith, in a way that we will attempt to specify further on, involves personal encounter. For this reason an understanding — a knowledge or science — of faith must resist too much abstraction. Personal encounters will not brook being abstracted. A and B have never had a personal encounter. It is always Eddie and Joe, Harvey, and Zelda. We may, of course, legitimately speak of having a "faith" in institutions — I believe in the American Constitution, the People's Republic, the Catholic Church — or a faith in doctrines — I believe in Science, in the Bhagavad-Gita, the teachings of the Apostles. But radically these uses of the term are ways of encapsulating a whole personal history, our own and others. Thus when we speak of "believing" or "having faith" in something, we are indicating that there is an emotionally toned investment of ourselves over and above what can be properly expressed in the word "know." One maintains a distance in knowledge which is not possible or desirable in faith. A foreign correspondent is the man to speak of "knowing" the People's Republic; a Chinese student "believes" in it. "Belief," "Faith," these are verbal gestures toward a very dense reality built often of many intersecting personal histories. In the case of the young Chinese patriot, his statement that he believes in the People's Republic is an affirmation of his experiences with family, friends, teachers and, above all, that running current of consciousness which is the sense of himself. So that he says in saying "I believe in the People's Republic" that the People's Republic is one of the living contexts in which he is able to identify his mother, say, as his mother, his friends for what they are to him, himself as he apprehends himself to be. A man will have many things he knows — the capital of Alaska, the specific gravity of copper, *The Darktown Strutters Ball* — many fewer things in which he believes. For a man in believing invests, commits himself and that he can do only a relatively few times.

We are all familiar with the *Saturday Evening Post* story: handsome young executive suddenly one day notices something about the elevator girl — crooked stocking seams, gamin grin (a standard gimmick) — she begins to come into focus, she has summoned his attention as a person and calls out to his own sense of himself as personal reality; after 5000 more words, a few minor mishaps and tirelessly pert exchanges between executive and girl, they marry. Just before we turn the page to read about the discouragement an ex-world series star is experiencing as a team manager, the deeper thinkers among us might pause to dwell for a moment or two on how impersonally we encounter elevator girls, supermarket checkout baggers, even taxicab drivers. It may occur to us that we are missing a good deal this way — each person is a microcosm richly endowed with thoughts and feelings which are not ours. How much more exciting and rewarding life would be if we dealt with them all on really significant levels. Yes, of course. But if we went around deliberately engaging every elevator girl in humorously erotic banter like the man in the story, we would find it an exhausting program and illegal as well.

On the other hand, having once allowed a human being to emerge in our consciousness as significant, we find the process hard to reverse. Indeed should someone insist that we do so, he can earn our just resentment. Picture the following dialogue:

"I love you."

"Inevitable, of course, that you should use that phrase. Did you know that there is statistical evidence that the phrase is spoken universally by English speakers at least once during the years of early adulthood, say, fourteen (I mean, naturally, biological adulthood) to — oh — twenty-five. Usually, as one would expect I suppose, it is addressed as you have just addressed it, to a member of the opposite sex."

"I love you."

"Universally! Isn't that amazing? There are practically no universal statistical patterns as you are well aware. But in this case it does seem the upper limit would prove out to be infinity."

The only possible ending of this little drama would be a sight gag (slap, kick, pie in the face) and blackout.

I am aware that the present line of argument can be and has been interpreted as a defense of irrationality. Despite the frivolity of my illustration, I intend nothing frivolous. It is probably impossible very precisely to define the relationship between faith and reason. What precision can be established is properly the task of theology. We can say here, however, that reason accompanies all faith, supports it, illuminates it, criticizes it. Doubtless a faith of some sort, in the sense of the giving of one's assent in excess of communicable evidence, accompanies all reasoning. As we have seen, insight precedes and controls in some measure the entire process of proof, even in the sciences. And the etiology of each insight is doubtless to be sought in the subjectivity of the man who experiences it. The theologian's commitment to reason is the source of that resentment we have seen which he receives constantly from believers. To many believers he can sound exactly like the exasperating pedant in our little dialogue. Speak the lover's lines, however, in a particularly goopey way, sighing from a sagging, overmoist mouth, and you have a decently accurate metaphor of the way many scientists and philosophers of science view the theologian's prior commitment to faith.

I suppose there is no final resolution of this problem. There is a decorum proper to intellectual work as there is to most things. There are styles — I think we may call them that — of the mind. The sciences pursue formal mental patterns wherever they may lead. At given points along his formal structures the scientist likes to drop plumb bobs into the world of sense experience; and if contact is established, he is assured of some control of concrete reality at that point and receives renewed confidence that his conceptual patterns are not without ontological relevance. Theology, from this point of view, is an impure science. It will not pursue mental patterns heedless, except at intermittent checkpoints, of the concrete experiences it seeks to understand. It feels its style of abstraction must be less severe than that of physics, or (although many theologians fail their own discipline here) metaphysics. Literary criticism, like theology, by and large refuses to abstract to the degree a purely scientific intention would have it do. The discipline of history seems divided between the pattern mongerers and old line humanists. The impact of the success of the physical sciences has been felt throughout the academic community and deserves to be. Theology, no less than other "nonscientific" disciplines can absorb a great deal of data from the physical sciences, can even design certain little projects of special interest to itself which can be quantified in the best scientific fashion, but it can never wholly adopt the methods of the sciences for that would be to ignore the qualities of things, the personally textured areas of reality where faith is generated and dwells.

THEOLOGY AND THE ENLIGHTENMENT

Humanism did not like it because it was abstract; science did not like it because it was concrete. Religion had never liked it because it was rationalistic. It can be no surprise that rationalism, when that movement of mind came to full flower in the eighteenth century, rejected theology because it was religious.

The really telling blows to theology's academic prestige, and the ones from which it suffers most even today, were delivered by the savants of the Enlightenment. The intellectual movements of the Renaissance which we have hastily reviewed here were not thought by their originators and advocates to be inimical to religion. Both humanist and scientist quarreled with established theological thought and method, as we have seen, but few members of either party felt called upon to attack religion as such. Quite the contrary, a great deal of the enthusiasm which both new movements stirred was connected with the religious convictions which animated the sixteenth and seventeenth centuries. Controversialists in all camps during that intensely religious and bellicose period summoned indiscriminately both the new science and the revival of ancient literature and learning to support their various positions. If it sometimes seems to us that the religious use of Renaissance learning was not distinguished by consistency, if we find Erasmus', Kepler's, Galileo's, Dryden's, Descartes' assertions that their central aim was to promote "true religion" —and all of them made such assertions — if we find these protests, rather than simple assertions, and shrill with the need to avoid pursuing their premises to their conclusions, we are reading the sixteenth and the seventeenth centuries in the light of the eighteenth. Religion, it was thought during the seventeenth century, could only be served by the new learning. Visions of God's ways justified to man, and of man and God reaching a new harmony and friendship in a fresh understanding of each other, were opening up on all sides. The theodicies fashioned by imitators of Descartes' purposes and methods, were not, as we have remarked, legitimate theologies since they willingly abandoned the real and messy world in which God has spoken his summons to faith for glittering worlds of geometric possibility. But neither were these theodicies, in their authors' intentions or in their immediate effect, philosophies fashioned as engines against religion. It was not merely professional Cartesians, such as Malebranche, who expected intellectual light and renewed religious fervor to result from Descartes' narrowly scientific and abstract rationalism but even professional ecclesiastics, such as Bossuet, could not perceive any intrinsic opposition to religion in the new thinking and were capable of expressing real enthusiasm for it. It is perhaps an instance where event creates logic, but after the Enlightenment it has become very hard for us to see how such positions were maintained without their advocates feeling the strain of paradox.

The Enlightenment is much too complicated a phenomenon both in its origins and structure but especially in its effects, for it to receive anything but the most cursory treatment in this essay. Essentially a movement of the bourgeois, engineered by men of very sufficient learning but of no great profundity whose aims were political rather than philosophical, whose talents were literary and synthetic even though they celebrated and used the achievements of science and rational analysis to work their purposes, the Enlightenment, it is no exaggeration to say, created the modern world. It is rare that history can legitimately see in an intellectual movement the shape and consistency of a party. The nature of language forces the historian, as well as everyone else, to speak of such movements as though they were produced by conscious partisans. And this essay, which does not pretend to be historically controlled, has offered an excellent instance, with its endless talk of "humanists" and "scientists" and "rationalists," of how much of the manifold of reality is lost behind such cavalier groupings and generalizations. But the men of the Enlightenment offer the clearest historical example of just a party. With surprisingly few exceptions they knew one another, and where they did not know one another they read, usually with approval, one another's work; and the degree to which they shared common purposes was little short of miraculous — despite miracles being something they had agreed to despise. For the chief work of the Enlightenment was the secularization of all aspects of European society and culture.

There have always been secularly minded men, even among theologians. Jean of Jandun concluded a long demonstration which proved that the doctrine of creation was a rational absurdity by adding flippantly that it should not, however, be considered too great a burden to believe it since "creation very seldom happens; there has never been but one, and that was a very long time ago."[20] If one cannot be justified in doubting Jean of Jandun's religious commitment, it does at least seem clear that he was no fanatic. Yet until the Enlightenment of the eighteenth century there was little opportunity for radical disbelief openly to express itself. Whatever secularistic dissent was present in the minds of learned men from the twelfth to the sixteenth centuries either was repressed or expressed only in ambiguous ways by men who were ordinarily theologians. And even in the seventeenth century the institutional articulations of religion were of such a fearful strength that Hobbes, whose *Leviathan* certainly witnessed to a dedicatedly mundane mind, felt the need to make his work oily with asservations of piety. Yet by the close of the eighteenth-century religion will have fallen into such a state of disrepute among the learned, that Schleiermacher in 1799 felt it necessary to address his book, *On Religion,* "to its cultured despisers."

It is of no use for our purposes to recount all of the ways by which the men of the Enlightenment undermined the seemingly impregnable power of the churches. They laughed at them, they sneered at them, they argued with them, they outmaneuvered them. And religion, through the errors of churchmen, through their high-handedness, their capacity to misread the times, through their alternate sycophancy and intolerance of the savants, cooperated in its own despite. The sectarian passions of the period of the religious wars and the amount of the blood which had been spilt in the name of orthodoxy were of recent memory and had become a mingled horror and shame to a Europe anxious for peace and anticipating (primarily from its exploitation of its colonies) prosperity. The abiding embarassment which Jeremy Bentham testifies to for his adolescent terror of ghosts can stand as a symbol both of the fatal intransigence with which the churches preached an archaic supernaturalism and of the intense reaction this preaching produced among the learned when at last they were disabused.[21]

The Enlightenment established the situation in which, with only minor changes, theology finds itself today. The patterns of belief and loss of

[20] Quoted from Hofstadter and Metzger, *op. cit.,* 35–36.
[21] Cf. *Memoirs of Bentham* in *The Works of Jeremy Bentham,* ed. John Bowring (New York: Russell and Russell, 1962), Vol. X, p. 18.

belief which environ its practice remain fairly much as the Enlightenment left them. If it is true, as this essay has presumed, that theology today must feel the need to defend its academic continuance, that need was created by *les philosophes* of the eighteenth century. Since with the Enlightenment we reach within the terms of this essay the modern period, we will abandon even that minimum of historical categorization we have used up to now. Rather, we will consider the various academic problems and options with which theology finds herself faced, under a series of systematic headings. Not all of theology's problems were present in the eighteenth century (except as a gleam in the eye of Voltaire); not all of the options were first presented then — much has happened, not least being that theology, under attack, has matured and grown stronger, subtler, much more deeply intellectual than it was. But in the rough and ready approximation to history we have been using up to now, it is true enough to say that the Enlightenment initiates, and rather completely anticipates, all the heavy weather through which the discipline of theology still makes its way.

THEOLOGY AND EPISTEMOLOGY

The most important problem theology needs to face in seeking to regain its rightful academic stature is epistemological. Epistemological questioning has been one of the most powerful instruments used by those who have destroyed theology's academic position, and anyone attempting to defend what remains of that position must try to answer for theology's epistemology.

The now classical objection to theology is to mock the pretensions implicit in its name, *theo-logos,* the study of God. "Presume not God to scan," wrote Alexander Pope, holding up, one imagines, his frail wrists for a moment to express a gentle horror before writing the cosily satisfied line: "The proper study of mankind is man." For an understanding of epistemological thought at least as it is pertinent to the criticism of theology, it is useful to pause a moment longer with the rationalists of the eighteenth century. For the most part, the men of the Enlightenment were deists, and it is in the sanctimoniousness which was felt to be the proper deistic attitude toward God that we have the pre-rational emotional matrix out of which theology's epistemological troubles arose.

In attempting earlier to vindicate the promethean nature of theological inquiry, I spoke — with some conscious theatricality — of men "burdened with the doubts and lonely fears . . . who would bring their

Maker to Judgment."[22] This is an image with which the deistic thinker could agree. "Precisely," he would say, "and that is why theology must be an affront to God." (It is amazing how frequently one unearths the fear of offering an affront to God. It unites both *philosophe* and humanist with the simple pious.) But in the picture of the tormented theologian I intended to evoke the man of faith whose moments of doubt and mental anquish are only moments in the theological inquiry. The audacity of a questioning faith can strike home strongly and be a fairly constant theme in one or another theologian's mind; and it is, no doubt, an occasional thought in the minds of all theologians. But it is only one of many possible reactions proper to the man of faith. Believing, accepting, trusting — these activities are always experienced as marbled with anxiety. Have I presumed? Will I be accepted? Have I acted too hastily? The questions arise inevitably whenever persons meet as persons, whether these be man and man, or man and God. Nevertheless, for the same reason, namely because in faith man meets God personally, the emotional spectrum attendant on the worship proper to one who believes in a personal and revealing God, is very large. It reaches from the mystic's ardors and audacities to the homey comfortableness of Sholom Aleichem's character, Teyve, in his dialogues with the Almighty — "Thanks, with Your help, I'm starving to death."

But the rationalist by definition is not a man of faith. He is a worshiper perhaps, and among the deists there were many worshipers whose earnestness and honesty no one has any warrant for doubting. But he is not a theologian and sees no need to become one, because unlike the theologian, the deist can prove his God. But what we can only prove, once the refined pleasures of the process itself are depleted, soon becomes uninteresting. As it is merely rationally perceived, it soon ceases to surprise. There is, of course, a narrow band of emotional reaction appropriate to the worship of a God who is the product of a rational proof. The "Great Architect of the Universe" certainly deserves a restrained respect and for more imaginative minds, the Supreme Technocrat can act as the source of a rather lively awe — "Dark Vortex of unplumbed power," that sort of thing. For the mathematically minded there is the satisfaction of the aesthetic appetite which arises from contemplating the God of rationalism as a reservoir of those infinities of infinites which are a mathematician's joys. But the available emotional range of the deist's worship is not large; and it all lies in the upper register of refinement near the

[22] Cf. above, p. 19.

limit of human perception. Such a God, like the 47th proposition of Euclid, a handsome and intricate work of the mind, soon becomes irrelevant to most of life. From irrelevance, to neglect, to doubt of his existence, makes an easy three-step gradation in the emotions. But doubting his existence becomes for the deist a doubt of the "proof" and thence, a doubt of the proving process. Pope's exhortation to theology, "Presume not God to scan," soon becomes, "How can you (or I or anyone) presume there is a God to scan?" With that question theology's epistemological troubles begin.

The epistemological problem can be divided into two questions which do, indeed, keep phasing each other in and out during actual epistemological reflection, but are nevertheless usefully distinguished in a systematic treatment of the matter. These are:

1. the problem of the origin of ideas. That is, how did the things which are in our minds get there?
2. the problem of verification. That is, how do we know that the things which are in our minds are actually the way things are in themselves?

Or, more simply: how do we know and how do we know that we know? The first of these two epistemological questions is all that we will be concerned with right now and we will try to keep the second from intruding for the present.

People who are interested in the epistemological question are usually possessed of the type of mentality which Bertrand Russell calls "simple-minded." He opposes such minds to the "muddle-headed," and considers himself "simple-minded." Simple-minded is a brilliantly chosen word for those he wishes to name; its wit encompasses both the strength and weakness of the class (Since "muddle-headed" can intend nothing but criticism, it is not — from my point of view, not Russell's — so happy a choice.) The simpleminded prefer to believe that all things are reducible to less complicated components. Sometimes they seem to have no sense of a lower limit to their power of reduction. Anything can always be seen to be nothing but two or three lesser things. "Nothing but," is one of their favorite phrases. Let me drift off for a moment in my muddle-headed way into autobiography. We will return, I hope, instructed.

I was once chided by a man who had some authority over me. His rebuke has remained with me longer than many other such rebukes (I have a large and varied collection and am by way of being a connoisseur) for reasons, I like to think, of its exemplary value. I had been out of doors on a cold March day. On meeting him after my return, I ventured the opinion that it was "a nice day."

"What do you mean 'a nice day?' It's cold, isn't it?"

"Yes, it's cold," said I, adding fecklessly, "but it's a sort of Spring-cold."

Now the temper of the conversation becomes earnest. His hunter instincts have been aroused. He had spied an imprecision and imprecisions were his meat. "What, young man," (he could say things like "young man,") is a "Spring-cold?"

"Well, it's cold all right. But there is a promise of warmth in the air." And for an impromptu answer to a very discombobulating question, I was foolish enough to think that would serve quite nicely.

"That may mean something to a poet. But it means nothing at all to a scientist. Cold is the absence of heat."

What is crucial to keep in mind here is that both of us were talking about knowing things. Or at least I thought I was. But my Gradgrindish interlocutor attempted, by using the word "poet," to push my observation out of the cognitive world entirely. Talk about "Spring-cold," he implied, was simply a verbal ornament, expressive merely, like wearing a funny hat or making a grimace. It was not descriptive of my experience of the day's weather at all. To attempt to rebut the implied statement that poets offer nothing of cognitive value would take us from our purpose. Whether I should have been considered a poet or not is beside the point. I thought I was expressing a cognitive experience in talking about a "Spring-cold;" furthermore, I was able concretely to discriminate a "Spring-cold" from other similar "colds." Why then was I suspected of simple dithering? Because whatever the element or elements were in my experience which moved me to express something over and above "the absence of heat," were not, as my critic saw the matter, objective, "in the air" as I claimed, but rather in myself. As for the phrase I had selected to express these elements, "a promise of warmth," it was beneath contempt. I was uttering only what I knew of myself — my expectation of warmer days — in every word except "cold." That was the single vocable which indicated the outside weather.

Now as an advocate and practicioner of muddleheadedness, it becomes incumbent upon me to recognize the many and great advantages which the simpleminded enjoy. First one notices a marvelous clarity to their thoughts and speech; when one has managed to get something said in the fashion approved by the simpleminded, it sounds really said.

The reason which I think most advocates of simpleminded forthrightness would use to explain their own practice, however, would be that simpleminded statements can be verified. Since the whole question of verification is something we shall examine much later in this essay this cannot be developed at the moment. We should only pause long enough to note that the simpleminded thinker may well be insisting on his method of breaking things into simple components or at least into *these* components rather than some others, not because they necessarily fit with his experience of the world but rather with his instruments of verification. Cold may well be considered "the absence of heat," not because we know it that way — men who die of freezing seem to feel a glow much like heat toward the end — but because our thermometers cannot record it in any other way.

But the great advantage which simpleminded thinkers have over the muddleheaded, an advantage particularly pertinent to the epistemological argument against theology, is that they manage to exclude the self from cognitive process. They are, as it is phrased, objective.[23] This quality of objectivity is, as we will state in a little while, not, in fact, very accessible. It was once thought that objectivity could be attained in such measure that the thinking which resulted would automatically produce truth. The source of these expectations seems to have been the success of the New Science at which we have glanced. We have already assigned that success to a willingness to mathematicize, to reduce "to the simplest terms." But as epistemologists read that success, it was to be attributed rather to what I prefer to see as an emotional accompaniment of mathematical thinking, namely disinterestedness.

From its beginnings the scientific community which emerged in the late Renaissance has been characterized by a previously unheard-of degree of unanimity. Philosophical, political, social problems persist unsolved for generations and little agreement can be reached concerning even the way these problems should be stated, let alone solved. The intellect seems in these areas to be as much an instrument of aggression as it is of reconciliation and harmony. Everyone's achieved knowledge is

[23] I do not, by any means, wish to imply that simpleminded thinkers in Russell's sense, by which he means those whose taste is for scientific abstraction and analysis, cannot make good theologians. Theologians, like the rest of the world, fall into divisions which can be named in Russell's terms. St. Thomas Aquinas was as simple-minded as Russell himself — and I suspect Russell would be willing to admit this. Teilhard and Rahner are muddleheaded compared with Lonergan and Von Balthasar. So it goes. The point of the discussion, however, is that theology, as a discipline, is muddleheaded as compared to, say physics . . . or at least that is the way Russell and likeminded epistemologists would see it.

achieved in despite of everyone else's. But scientists appear to go from strength to strength, and problem-solving among them is a cooperative enterprise which results in more or less peacefully shared control. No epistemologist since the successes of Galileo and Kepler has been able to ignore this marvelous scientific unanimity so unprecedented in intellectual history. Seemingly every theory of knowledge sets as its goal to prescribe for all the disciplines a way of thinking which will produce agreement similar to that of the scientists. It is my conviction that the essential reason why science is able to maintain unanimity is not to be sought so much in its special method of thinking, but rather in the object of its study, namely experience so abstracted that it goes beyond the level where insight abounds.

Men *need* to know about ethics and politics, their social relations and their arts, what they know (or think they do) is very important to them. Consequently, they proliferate ideas and conceptual frameworks in these matters and defend them vigorously. Nature — star and molecule alike — is too inert and remote in human consciousness, especially after it has been reduced to the simplicity required by the mathematicizing sciences, to generate much partisan feeling. Men are content to work within a few agreed-upon frameworks. The temptation to contentiousness is simply not as strong in the sciences as it is in the humanities. Disinterest, the hallmark of the scientific temper, more easily comes to be where greater lack of interest is possible.[24]

Now again, in saying this I am not by any means attempting to attack the sciences. This disinterest has had the most happy results. Cooperative and industrious, the sciences have, with relatively few major revolutions, maintained a kind of intellectual peace which has been enormously productive. What I am saying is that it can be doubted that they have, beyond their willingness to reduce conscious experience to the bare minimals necessary for abstraction, offered anything specifically original to the cognitive process. This of course, may legitimately be considered quite original enough. But by and large simpleminded epistemologists have not thought so. Indeed in envy of the serenity of the sciences they

[24] Thomas S. Kuhn's *The Structure of Scientific Revolutions* (Phoenix Books, The University of Chicago Press, 1962), is my source for most of these remarks. This most remarkable and original work is one I shall have cause to cite again. He has with great courage and pertinacity of vision placed scientific thought into its actual human context. No more than he, would I contend that his historical and phenomenological reading of scientific thought has rendered the many "philosophies of science" otiose. But it certainly should force some radical revisions.

erected the attainment of disinterest into almost the single purpose of their analysis of knowledge. Phenomenal experience always so cluttered with emotion must be ruthlessly criticized until no chance survives that the subject's own interests should effect his perception of the object. This is the source of what Wittgenstein calls the Cartesian noetic model: the ghost in the machine,[25] where the mind, all its confusions methologically reduced to the patterned order of "clear and distinct" ideas, imperturbably surveys the busy universe (including, of course, itself) proceeding on frictionless rails. The world becomes machine in this model of knowledge, not because it is experienced that way, so much as because, seeing it that way, the "angelic" mind can maintain its serenity. If the world remains that mess of pain and delight the conscious subject knows in his unabstracted experience, there can be little scientific disinterest. Subjectivity can be no better rebuked than by turning the objects which elicit it into mere mechanisms. When knowledge and love, justice and appetite, become no more interesting than clockworks and ball bearings, the mind can be at peace. Listen to how painfully and exactly a simpleminded thinker seeks to bleach out all subjectivity from his discourse:

> Being a sense datum, or sensum, is a relational property of the item which is sensed. To refer to an item which is sensed in a way which does not entail that it *is* sensed, it is necessary to use some other locution. *Sensible* has the disadvantage that it implies that sensed items could exist without being sensed, and this is a matter of controversy among sense-datum theologists. *Sense content* is, perhaps, as neutral a term as any.[26]

Neutrality, the search for neutrality — that is the aim of all knowledge. The neutral word, the neutral attitude, the neutral judgment, and the neutral experiment, these are the tools of the man who knows. Prejudice, self-seeking, bias, dishonesty, these insidious manifestations of the self must be manfully disciplined out wherever the alert attention of a real thinker detects them. A wonderful and exalted ideal — no wonder that Jacob Bronowski can envision building a whole ethics

---

[25] Cf. Gilbert Ryle, *The Concept of Mind* (London: Hutchinson, 1949), p. 8. Later publications of the "Oxford School" have attributed the origin of the phrase to Wittgenstein.

[26] The quotation, which is simply exemplary, is from Wilfrid Sellars, "Empiricism and the Philosophy of Mind," in *Minnesota Studies in the Philosophy of Science*, Vol. I, eds. by Herbert Feigel and Michael Scriven (Minneapolis: University of Minnesota Press, 1956), p. 254.

on the practice of scientists.[27] Theology alone of all the disciplines seems not to have caught this vision. With a quiet complacency theology admits it does not even have an object of study except in faith, except, that is, in an inherently subjective way.

The *theos*, the God, of theology is obviously not an object in the same sense as the earth is for geology, as men, their races and customs, are for anthropology as the forms of life are for biology. God is not an object out in front of the senses which is to be studied and tested. Nor is there any argument to be made against the epistemological criticisms of theology by pointing out that such studies as psychology and, indeed, epistemology itself, also have intangible objects. It is not the intangibility of theology's *theos* which is the source of complaint (except in the systems of the most hardshelled empiricists). It is rather the manner in which the theologian comes to know his object of study and the treatment and testing to which he subjects it. For all the disciplines of the mind, except theology, strive to treat their objects, *as* objects, to create and maintain a distance between the knower and what he knows, even when the thing known is, as in the case of epistemology, knowledge itself. Theology, it is argued, on the contrary, never even attempts objectivity. It makes the act of subjective faith a precondition for the discipline; it eschews neutrality from the beginning. Since this is so, it is simply pointless to consider it seriously as a rational discipline of the mind.

These objections are not without point even today. But they are much less telling than they formerly were, when a naïve empiricism controlled most epistemological thinking. Pure empiricism is almost nowhere any longer maintained. The pure percept, thoroughly uncontaminated with concept, is thought today even by strict behaviorists to be unattainable; and if it could be experienced it would probably prove nearly useless, noetically speaking. The rationalistic model of knowledge which proposed a chastened and disciplined subjectivity, passive as a silver emulsion to the light of objective reality, is now widely admitted to be mistaken. As we saw, even in the strictly experimental practice of science, no one can be sure that his results do not carry some subjective taint. Now once it is seen that a conceptual framework of some kind accompanies all apprehension, it is impossible

---

[27] Cf. J. Bronowski, *Science and Human Values* (New York: Harper Torchbooks, 1956), *passim* but esp. the final chapter, "The Sense of Human Dignity," p. 63 ff.

to think of knowing as a process that produces knowledge as a sausage machine does sausage, by being distant, uninvolved, and different. Rather, knowing is creating a symbiosis between knower and known, much as sausages produce bones, by becoming them. Much as, or, better, somewhat as. For the bones so totally dominate their nutriment in the achieved state of unity that the sausages are not even a shadow of their former selves. It was thought, after the Humean and Kantian critiques of knowledge, that something like that would have to be the final metaphor for our understanding of our own thoughts, that subjectivity so transformed the manifold of objects that nothing of them as themselves, useful for true knowledge, could be said to remain. We had no assurance that the transforming process of knowledge did not distort what we knew beyond the point of genuine usefulness. Except, of course, that we could and did use them — to build bridges and air conditioners, improve toothpaste and dissuade people from suicide. The success of technology has enabled us to endure without despair our confinement in the cell of our own subjectivity to which a purely rational analysis of thinking would continually confine us.

The present state of the problem, as I read it, is such that some impatience with it has a color of justification. It may be that like Archimedes asking for "a lever and a place to stand," we have posed ourselves an impossible problem in the very conditions we demand for its solution. For, if Heisenberg can argue that any observation affects the unobserved state of the object under scrutiny, this is all the more true, if we are attempting by reflection to observe our own mental processes. It seems to me that anyone interested in epistemology today has abandoned (or would do well to abandon) the pristine formulation of it which is roughly the same as we placed above under our first question: how do we know? A single "origin for our ideas" has never been less determinable. We seemed to have reached a kind of intellectual consensus that we do not know with any remarkable degree of precision how "the things which are in our minds got there," and that we probably never will. Since, then, we are to be bilked of finding a single process, it is pointless to look for *the* right way to carry on the process. There is no prescription for right thinking except to think. There is no way to produce insight under controlled conditions. One must by means that are doubtless deeply private, secreted even from the conscious mind, strive to experience the nonself in one's self — to think — and be prepared to endure the partiality of the results. (One must also of course, be ready to submit the results, his ideas, to whatever means of verification are at hand, but that comes under our second question and is another story.)

It is consequently, at least unfair to banish theology from the intellectual commonwealth on the grounds that its concepts arise out of faith. For all conceptualizations are in some sort the results of the commitment of the person, of the knowing subject, and this commitment, if it is not a commitment to belief, is something very much like it. (Again it should be remembered that we are attempting to leave all considerations of verification out of the account in this section.) There is no such a thing as a neutral idea. If any idea exists, it is the product of someone's commitment of himself to its making. What we mean by neutrality in intellectual work is not so much a chastening of the self as it is a willingness to do what we saw Galileo doing, abstract. To support these assertions it may prove useful to return to our little exemplary story. Perhaps we may be able to make it a cautionary tale for overconfident epistemologists.

My critic and I were both talking about the weather. This is a noun which denominates a rather complex area of fact. Atmosphere, relative positions of sun and earth (and the rest of the solar system, for all either of us knew), degree of earth rotation, amount of ozone and a plethora of other chemicals in the air matrix; the number of variables could quickly be seen to be one approaching infinity if one wanted to, as we say, "stop and think." In addition it should be noted that there is a high antiseptic gloss to the kind of thinking preferred by my friend as well as to the language in which he expresses himself, which is in its own way very gratifying. Not only is it satisfactorily destructive ("Take that, young man!" Whack.) but it is so elaborately finical that it manages to appear at once as unassailable as a fortress, while being neat as an egg. If you think I am trying to suggest that there are possible noncognitive motives for preferring the apparently neutral locutions of the simpleminded, that esthetic considerations might be at work or even more blatant kinds of self-indulgence, you are perfectly correct. For my critic, no more than I, could be sure that my perception of a "spring-cold" was without foundation in fact; and his refusal to grant that was a way of shutting off further investigation as effectively as turning on his heel and walking off.

Essentially what was happening was that two different kinds of knowers, in Russell's terms, confronted each other. It should however, be clear by now that these are carelessly denominated different *kinds* of knowers. Knowledge happens within all knowers in roughly the same unknown ways. What meaningfully differentiates one knower from another is rather what they each choose to recognize as important in the manifold of experience. The simpleminded and muddleheaded differ from one another by their willingness to abstract from the unrefined density of experience in search of that power over experience we call knowledge. The first kind of knower is very willing to abstract; the second much less so. What the simpleminded gain is clarity, confidence, precision; what they lose is range and significance. The muddleheaded may indeed be just what Russell meant their name to imply, but their advantage over their counterparts is that their refusal to abstract to the same degree as the simpleminded, leaves them struggling in obscurity often enough, but struggling to express what is humanly meaningful. It is fair to say that in the present state of knowledge theory "you pays your money and you takes your choice."

THEOLOGY AND AUTHORITY

Although the present state of epistemological thinking admits subjective preference to be an important, perhaps determining element in all thought, even the most highly rational, why is it that theology, by insisting that it arises out of faith, has been largely unable to regain its lost academic prestige? It would be bitterly ironical that theology should be faulted for being the only discipline to recognize the truth about its own methods. Yet it is true that most academicians who wish to prevent theology from returning to a honored place among university disciplines will argue against the subjectivity of faith as though a knowledge bleached of subjectivity were as possible as the rationalists believed it to be. On the other hand, in addition to the crimes against the intellect, which many see theology and those committed to theological thinking to have been historically guilty of, there is the impression that theology acts too flaccidly and supinely in face of the subjective threat. It may be well and good to recognize that all knowledge takes place in a subjective context and retains a subjective dimension; and theology, basing itself on faith, may be doing nothing but what all disciplined thinking does in basing itself on conviction. But theology might well be less complacent about it. One of the crucial instances of theology's complacent acquiescence to subjectivity is, as its enemies see it, its constant toadying to authority.

Stephen C. Pepper's *World Hypotheses* offers a particularly brilliant instance of an argument against theology which borrows its real strength from the distaste the author can presume his readers to feel for theology's "authoritarianism."[28] It is unfortunate that the formalisms which this essay has assumed do not permit me to speak at this point as enthusiastically as I would prefer to of Mr. Pepper's book. Although it was not in fact the generating source of many of my own insights into the radically subjective nature of scientific thinking, *World Hypotheses* corroborates my opinions very satisfactorily — a state of affairs that would in the natural course of things issue in enthusiasm. However, the book illustrates too aptly the hidden dimension of antitheological bias which lies behind many seemingly cool analyses of theology's "hopeless" commitment to authoritarian thinking. Reluctantly I consign him for the moment to the role of villain.

The central thesis of *World Hypotheses* is that any large-minded thinking about the universe will inevitably shape itself around one or more "root metaphors." The metaphors that have actually enjoyed wide cultural currency are quite limited in number. Pepper finds only four to be capable of generating "relatively adequate" world views or hypotheses. These are "formism" (the world as similarly shaped), "mechanism" (the world as machine), "contextualism" (the world as event in space-time), "organicism" (the world as total organism). These descriptions, especially in the last two cases, fundamentally distort the careful subtlety of Pepper's thought. Yet, although this remains regrettable, it is not important for our immediate purpose. For, in addition to these four "relatively adequate hypotheses," he adds two more as illustrations of very "inadequate world hypotheses." It is these which concern us for both are peculiarly proper to the theologian's way of thought.

The first "very inadequate world hypothesis" he calls Animism, in which the world is seen as human person. This root metaphor he finds inadequate because it is unable to explain, to render cognitively clear the facts of human experience. The only kind of clarity Pepper admits, however, tells against this metaphor from the beginning and seems rather to be defined in line with his own preferences than to offer an analysis of actual human knowing. Thus, he says that to see the world through the metaphor of the human person is to see it without any real precision. "This lack of precision [shows] itself either in an inability

28 *World Hypotheses* (Berkeley and Los Angeles: University of California Press, 1961).

to come to close quarters with a fact (that is, cognitive vagueness), or in an overability to produce interpretations of a fact any one of which would be as consistent with the categories as any other (that is, cognitive indeterminateness) . . . ."[29]

This, to speak concretely, seems to say that it is not useful to ask the question, "Who is thundering?" when one wishes to control thunder. The question, "What is thunder" has in fact been more productive of lightening rods and cloud-seeding planes than "Who?" In this way the personal metaphor has demonstrated its "inability to come to close quarters with a fact." This is all true from some aspects and yet may well be insignificant for a judgment on the final cognitive value of the root metaphor of the world as person. For it presumes that same restricted area of cognitive interest which we have seen again and again to lie behind those theories of knowledge which have been wielded as antitheological engines. It presumes that the power to verify—in empirical fashion — e.g., Franklin's key and spark — is the one credible litmus of fact. It presumes indeed other root metaphors, particularly perhaps the mechanistic. If we travel vertically away, however, in either direction from the level of experience where the world-as-machine operates best we meet the relevance of the world as person reasserting itself. When the relatively massive phenomenon of lightning is microscopically considered, we find ourselves faced with hordes of particles whose behavior is remarkably analogous to that of men in the mass.[30] And so too, ascent from the level of experience favored by the mechanists only confronts us with the Who-question much more urgently. Once the simplicities of strict animism have been bypassed (and despite Mr. Pepper's implications to the contrary those who favor the world-person root metaphor are not logically mired in a mythopoetic world of many spirits) the question, "Who is thundering?" reasserts itself. One does not need to believe in the Spirit of Thunder to query whether thunder may not ultimately be willed. The objection to the world-

[29] *Ibid.*, p. 118.

[30] I have no further purpose in mind here than to point out the metaphorical aptness of the world as person to the conceptual framework in which the natural sciences today treat of elementary particles. This has been done before; for the similarities are very arresting. The unpredictable behavior of designated particles, joined with the statistical regularity of the macroscopic clouds, so remarkably parallels human behavior that it must occur to anyone who studies the matter. I am not suggesting that the metaphor could be of use to the natural sciences, but I should like to insist that the possibility of its proving cognitively useful in the future cannot be ruled out because it has not been so up to now.

person metaphor which Pepper phrases as "cognitive indeterminacy" seems to be nothing but typical "simpleminded" impatience with the richness of experience which was what forced us to deal with it metaphorically in the first place. It is Descartes' Euclidean model of consistent, invariant comprehension that lies behind this objection, and since the entire tenor of *World Hypotheses* is to make evident the inadequacy of such restricted models, this objection is all the more ungrateful coming from its author.

The second "very inadequate" world view Mr. Pepper treats of he calls Mysticism and assigns as its root metaphor, the world-as-love. Pepper's objection here is that, while the experience of love is cognitively precise and eminently factual, it is limited in scope and consequently fails to do what it set out to do, *viz.* explain the universe of fact. Since the mystical experience is exalted, unified and intense, hatred, division, and boredom, the prose of life, must be excluded from any world hypothesis taking love as its root image. The mystic-lover does not explain these but simply banishes them to nothingness; he calls them unreal.

Here it seems to me Mr. Pepper's knowledge of the intention of actual mystical teaching is deficient — at least as that applies to Christian mystics. Pain, hatred, misery, all find place in the various syntheses of mystical Christianity. It is true that often these are seen metaphysically as proper to the becoming of the world rather than to its being, and so less "real," by which appellation however the mystics do not deny the factual (in Pepper's sense, *i.e.*, experienced) existence of such things. It would indeed be strange if a view that the world is radically love, which view was sustained by belief in the Crucified, could be proved to have no room for pain.

Furthermore, fundamental to Pepper's rejection of mysticism as a world hypothesis is his suspicion of love's cognitive value.

> Every lover believes his beloved to be the most perfect and beautiful creature in the world. We expect every lover to have that conviction. We smile at his illusion, wish him his full and happy indulgence of it, make our own cognitive corrections and expect him to do the same at a sober time. The feeling of cognitive certainty which normally accompanies the emotion is discounted as cognitive evidence for anything beyond the intensity and sincerity of the emotion. Under the conditions there is no cognitive problem . . .[31]

[31] *World Hypotheses,* p. 31.

That illusions such as described here occur, that they are often accompanied by a powerful emotional experience frequently denominated "love," no one can deny. That such illusions inevitably are generated by strong emotion, that illusion-generating emotion is what the mystic has in mind as the root metaphor of the world of his vision, these are by no means necessary conclusions. Even fairly pedestrian love-experience can claim cognitive accomplishments. A lover "sees" in the beloved potentialities *and* deficiencies to which a non-lover is blind. The seer-lover is at least as frequently encountered as his opposite number, the stereotyped "poor fool." Insight as often issues from an aroused sensibility as illusion does. Much as I would like to break another lance or two in the defense of love as root-metaphor for a world vision, it would delay us even longer in this aside with Pepper's book which is already quite long enough. Let us simply assert that it should be possible for the reasons adumbrated here to find that Mr. Pepper's conviction that these two root-metaphors, the world as person and the world as love, are "very inadequate," is based less on his analysis of their inherent limitations than he claims, and much more on his prior rejection of them for reasons which lie outside the metaphors themselves. These reasons are discernible and are, I believe, connected with the fear, shared by others besides Mr. Pepper, of theology's commitment to authority.

For the rejection of these two root metaphors is in fact rejection of Christian theology. The theologian must strive to give intellectual utterance to the faith expressed in St. Paul's letter to the Colossians[32] that Christ is form and image of all creation. Nor is his faith adequately expressed by seeing in the Pauline texts an ethical meaning only, that is, an exhortation to make whatever is under our control more luminously witness to the Divine desire to be revealed in human life; the intention of the Christian belief in Christ as the form of the cosmos expressed in Colossians, is clearly ontological. Thus to know the world is for the Pauline Christian to know Christ; for the world in some manner *is* Christ. If the root-metaphor of the world-as-person is "inherently inadequate," the Christian theological enterprise is corrupt at its source. The same is true of the world-as-love, since the essential Christian beliefs in Creation, Predestination, and Providence all suppose the will of God to be the central cosmic dynamism. But the antitheological bias of Pepper's argument that these two root metaphors

[32] Col 1:15–20.

are inherently inadequate becomes very clear in his insistence that the world-as-person will necessarily support its claim to be a cosmic root metaphor by an appeal to an Infallible Authority (his capitals); and the world-as-love must rest on an arrogant assumption of certainty.

It is precisely the history of theological thinking, as that history is read in and through the categories which were developed for the destruction of theological thinking, which Pepper has erected into a metaphysic.[33]

The purpose of this interlude with Mr. Pepper's *World Hypotheses* has been to illustrate how even a recent epistemologist whose sophistication is unquestioned can persist in an academic contempt for theology and this despite an intellectual temper palpably irenic. Mr. Pepper knows that radically all thinking is an instrument for self-expression that the patterning of experience we call argument is ultimately the result of insight, that insight is generated where will and intellect meet. Here is the ground of his "root metaphor" analysis. But his large charity to a plurality of deep preferences does not extend to the cognitive choices of Christian theologians because he fears their choice must imply a commitment to authoritarianism. And there has emerged one permanent result at least from the epistemological investigations of the past two hundred years. Epistemology has been unable to discover a model for "objective" thought, but it is sure that no genuine thinker can allow himself to be confined within authoritarian bounds. It was once anticipated that if man could not be sure that he knew the world of the nonself as it was to itself, not as it was to him, no option except a skepticism, timorous, bitter or armored in frivolity, was open to him. But rather than being despairing, the general mood among epistemologists as well as among researchers and theoreticians in all branches of knowledge, is high-hearted. Knowledge can never be final, that is all. Once it is seen that selected conceptual frameworks of some sort accompany all apprehen-

---

[33] I would like to reiterate my very great admiration both for the insights of *World Hypotheses* and the elegance and rigor with which they are argued. I must not be understood as contending that either of the metaphors Pepper rejects are, in the present state of knowledge, actually "adequate." It is an ironical fact of intellectual history that Mechanism, say, has yielded more useful information even in psychology than a personalist world hypothesis. We have no warrant to reject the knowledge which the other four world views offer because we are not naturally led to them by Christian belief. On the other hand, because these points of view which are essential to Christian theological thinking *have* not been usefully employed in the cognitive exploration of large areas of experience gives us no warrant to insist they cannot — at least, as I hope I have shown, on the arguments presented in *World Hypotheses*.

sion, that our ideas effect the way we know things, then we must be ready, if we wish to pursue truth, to change our ideas, that is all. We must be, in the jargon to the day, "open to new ideas." But this healthy spirit of revisionism seems to be lacking in theology. Here is one discipline which values originality less than it values tradition and authority.

The partisan loyalties we saw emerging from the Enlightenment still remain fierce and unqualified. What is theology to do? It is a disciplinary necessity for theology to revere authority. Should it, nevertheless, in order to win back its lost academic prestige, to lose the stigma of authoritarianism, abandon its reverence for authority, or conceal it? These questions are particularly crucial in Catholic theology and are so important an issue as Catholic theology faces the judgments of the intellectual world in the present day that they deserve a separate treatise. We at least shall dignify the issue by placing it under its own headline.

THEOLOGY AND TRADITION

In the word "faith" two intentions can be discerned. The first is clear in such a context as, "the teaching of the faith," and refers to the doctrinal content of a given religious position. Thus if the Methodist Church teaches its adherents that it is wrong to drink, the evil of drink becomes part of the *faith*, according to this first intention of the word. The second intention is associated with the adjectival forms of the word, faithful, faithfulness, and refers most immediately to ways of acting. A Methodist being exhorted not to drink is being told to "keep the *faith*" in this second sense. At the time of the Reformation a good deal of misunderstanding was generated through a confusion between these two intentions of the word. For Luther and his followers *faith*, so crucial an element in the Gospel teaching and especially the letters of St. Paul, names the essential element in salvation, *viz.* God's creating a loyal love of himself in the minds and hearts of the redeemed. Catholics preferred to reserve the word for an emphasis within the totality of salvation, namely the intellectual, the credal. Protestants tended to use the word in the second of its two intentions; Catholics in the first. Yet, the intentions are closely allied. It is not surprising that they have been associated with the same word in many languages.

Two intimate friends find in their friendship a way of knowing each other that the rest of the world beyond their circle of intimacy could never claim to have. Furthermore the depth of their insight is in function of the fidelity of their friendship. "Eddie could never do that," is a proposition which can only be assented to with firm certitude by Eddie's intimates. Former friend, we say, no longer "knows" former friend. The knowledge which arises from insight generated by love is always suspect, of course, by the "simpleminded" who would like to be able to precipitate out the purely cognitive factors from the loving-knowing solution. But personal knowledge, that is, of persons and between persons and which is, in addition, the expression of persons, must resist abstraction to simpler states. It remains stubbornly muddleheaded.

Take the situation of a man who is asked to doubt the fidelity of his wife. Until the demand is made — a barroom taunt, say — he is "blissfully happy." This is the situation exactly which W. H. Auden imagines in the section of his verse drama, *For the Time Being*, entitled "The Temptation of St. Joseph."[34] What is such a man to do? Presuming that he has his reasons, densely private and incommunicable as they may be, he can do nothing, except perhaps to knock his taunter down. In the circumstances that would be a highly intelligent course of action. But he cannot investigate the matter as a neutral observer and hope to come up with the truth. Should he achieve a state of impassivity in which he can apply a methodological doubt, immediately all the evidence he has for his wife's fidelity begins to look shabby. What, after all, has he got to go on? Looks, gestures, tone of voice? Yet these are all the evidence which really tell the truth of the matter. He may be sure of her because, to a degree unrecognized by himself, he needs to be and in his need he reads her as being much more loving than she is in fact. She may be an accomplished actress. All of this may or may not be true. The only available evidence remains the same. Given that in fact she is faithful and loving, she has no other means of demonstrating it that are available to the talented deceiver. And her husband must believe faithfully in her fidelity in order to be sure she is faithful. Any other course would be highly unreasonable of him, much as it may appear "rational" to a third observer. Again the presumption is that he has no reason in his own experience to doubt her, except the demand made on him from outside.

Now there is no reason why he could not tell his wife about the incident, question her, inquire. But if he conducts an "investigation" — by which word I mean here to connote an inquiry made in a cooly rational manner which, since it is seeking to establish love, banishes love from the inquiry — detectives, cross examinations, all that. Not only may he so

34 Printed in *Religious Drama I* (New York: Meridian Books, 1957).

affect his wife's attitude that the infidelity which in fact was not present before, becomes at least a real possibility, but he will also find that his greed for reassurance devours *all* evidence. He suspects shrewdly and coldly and without intermission; and his suspicions rage down all protests. The stance of the impartial observer is ideally suited to discover infidelity; it is almost totally incapable of confirming a fidelity which is factually present. Unless the husband is willing to let his "love for her, tuck him up and kiss goodnight,"[35] unless he is willing loyally to believe her loyal, he can never know she is.

The two intentions of the word faith operate together. What is faithfully known is the knowledge which is not otherwise available except in faith. This is true of all instances where knowledge demands as precondition for its coming to be a commitment to the truth of itself on the part of the one seeking to have the knowledge. We have seen that something of that works in all cognition even where it is most impersonal and distant from specifically human concern. But on the dense, unabstracted level where men conduct such quintessentially human activities as loving and worshiping, whatever knowledge *is* obtainable insists imperiously on personal fidelity. One is not allowed to know in mind what is not already known in heart. Mind and heart, of course, support and influence each other. Faith in the sense of knowledge is made possible by faithful faith, and feeds in turn the faith which feeds it. Since our concern is with religious faith and religious knowledge, we can most usefully illustrate this relationship between the two attitudes which are named in the two intentions of the word faith, by instancing the Bible.

H. Richard Niebuhr suggests the eighth Psalm as an example of how intricate the two faiths are to each other.[36]

> When I behold your heavens, the work of your fingers, the moon and the stars which you have set in place —
> What is man that you should be mindful of him, or the son of man that you should care for him? —
> You have made him little less than the Angels, and crowned him with glory and honor.
> You have given him rule over the works of his hands, putting all things under his feet:
> All sheep and oxen, yes, and the beasts of the field,

[35] *Ibid.*, p. 29.

[36] H. Richard Niebuhr, *Radical Monotheism and Western Culture* (New York: Harper and Brothers, 1960), pp. 13–14. Niebuhr uses the Psalm for much the same purpose as I do, though our readings differ in detail and emphasis.

The birds of the air, the fishes of the sea, and whatever swims
the path of the seas.
O Lord, our Lord, how glorious is your name over all the earth.

First it should be noted that in this "humanistic" celebration of man
the author's attitude is complex and paradoxical. The work of God is so
splendidly huge that man is humbled, but it is precisely the splendor of
man which is the crown of the God's work. It is then difficult to assign a
single central proposition to the Psalm, but certainly toward the center of
the piece's meaning we find something which we can phrase as "man is
the ruler of creation." This knowledge is arrived at by a review of
evidence. Man's ability to hunt and domesticate the rest of the terrestrial
animals witnesses to the truth of the proposition. A modern religious
thinker might be moved to the same conclusion by the larger cranial
capacity and greater convolutions of the human brain, or by a review
of the technological accomplishments of the race.[37] Yet in using the
phrases we just have, "move to a conclusion," "arrive at knowledge," we
are, of course, borrowing from the linear metaphor which is customarily
used in describing the process of reasoning. The movement of the psalmist's mind is obviously, however, circular, rather than linear. All his
evidence points radially in toward the central knowledge — that he is
loved and honored by the Creator — which in turn is experienced as
preceding and even giving rise to the evidence by which it is illuminated.
It is not that the knowledge which arises out of faith is exempted from
the logical prohibition against circular reasoning. It is simply that logic
can never claim to be more than a part of the process of the knowing
which is proper to faith. The believer can be logical, and when he is,
he is bound to the rules of logic; but logic is never more than instru-
mental and subordinate in the demonstration of the truths the believer
holds. The total proof is larger than logic can either contain or express.
It is felt as well as known, perceived as well as uttered. The psalmist
here is possessed of his knowledge before he finds reasons for it, at least
reasons available for utterance; and the reasons borrow their persuasiveness from the knowledge they make evident.

In all of this I am not precisely trying to vindicate such knowledge
against the accusations of its detractors. We are still not prepared to
discuss the means by which faith-knowledge can be verified, and must

[37] An antireligious thinker, of course, might employ much the same material to
establish an article in the secular creed: *e.g.*, "Man is so great, who needs God?" In
any case the movement of his mind would follow a similar pattern to that followed
by the psalmist.

postpone the question once again until later on in the essay. What I have been trying to do is to establish that the two senses of faith reinforce each other. Faith-knowledge must go hand in hand with faith-fidelity in order to be the knowledge it is. The theologian, then, both because his material is faith-knowledge and the knowledge that he seeks of it is further faith-knowledge, must be richly endowed with faith-fidelity if he hopes to be successful. This is a condition of his discipline, not primarily, as we are discussing it here, a matter of personal morality for the theologian. In the concrete, of course, it is probably both. Nevertheless, as one would expect in a discipline as ancient as theology, the intellectual and moral virtues necessary for its academic health have become institutionalized throughout the centuries. There exist today disciplinary expressions of the necessary virtues. The theologian must, in order to be seriously considered by his academic peers, express the fidelity necessary to make possible the kind of knowledge he seeks by working within theological tradition.

Any discipline may be spoken of either as the body of doctrine it possesses or as the group of speculators and researchers who are attempting to enlarge that body of doctrine. Interestingly enough, those disciplines which emphasize the existence and secure possession of a body of doctrine, those then which are intellectually conservative in the sense that they are unwilling to change their approach to the problems of their material in any radical manner without a good deal of difficulty, are, paradoxically, the very disciplines which show little regard for the concept of "tradition" in the sense that it used in theology and the humanities. Thus, one can imagine a useful member of the present-day discipline of chemistry who is able to make really sound contributions to the knowledge of his fellow researchers but who had never heard the name Dalton in his life and whose knowledge of Dalton's work is confined totally to what is implied in the working postulates of modern chemists. The physical scientists, who must necessarily emphasize the body of disciplined knowledge possessed by each of them in common with his colleagues over the men who acquire and extend that body, feel little need to pause and gather authorities and precedents about them in order to gain the attention of their fellow scientists. Since they steadfastly presume the continuity of their discipline they feel small need to look backward. The case is quite otherwise in the humanities. Few literary critics would allow themselves to plead ignorance of Dryden or Arnold and expect to be taken seriously by other literary critics. The humanities have emerged in the course of this essay as those disciplines which are characterized by a reluctance to abstract too far from the manifold of human experience. They are, consequently, suspicious of the merely formally elegant idea, and value their own histories as an account more of thinkers than of thoughts. In this sense they are, in relation to the disciplinary preferences of the sciences, fonder of tradition.

But the theologian respects tradition, is willing patiently to explore writings of his predecessors, to weigh their opinions against his own, not merely because he recognizes along with his fellow humanistic thinkers that the materials derived from human experience are, in the relatively unabstract manner in which the humanistic disciplines deal with them, very impervious to the schematizations of the conceptualizing mind, not merely for these reasons does he respect tradition, but because, as we saw, consultation of theological tradition is the disciplinary expression of that fidelity which must accompany the knowledge of faith which he seeks. These conditions would prevail in the theology of any kind of theologian. It is a little abstract to speak this way, since the question we are concerned with, of the academic status of theology, is raised in the actual framework of Western intellectual history and pertains in fact to Judeo-Christian theologians; nevertheless, a healthy respect for tradition would be a necessary condition for a Buddhist or Taoist theologian and even for a secularist theologian, could such a creature come to be. All of these would need to consult carefully and earnestly the opinions of others who believe as they do in order to treat in a genuinely theological manner their common faith. But the Christian theologian is bound to tradition in excess even of the degree to which theologians as a class would be bound. For the Christian theologian is an investigator of Christian belief, and one of the tenets of that belief is that it arises not from human insight but from the gift of God. It is revealed.

THEOLOGY AND REVELATION

The rhetorical strategy we have adopted in this essay has been to support theology's claims to be restored to an honored place in the academic world by indicating how little its methods and intentions differ from those of other academic disciplines. Now, this is clearly more than merely a rhetorical stratagem. It expresses my own convictions concerning the nature of thinking and especially concerning the nature of that cognitive forum we call the academy or university.[38] When serious think-

[38] An abstraction, of course, since the "academy" lacks local habitation if not a

ing is concretely, or perhaps it would be more accurate to say phenome-
nologically, examined, it all becomes roughly the same enterprise: an
attempt to reduce the swarm of conscious experience to order usually
for the purposes of control. The attempt is pursued, as I see it, along
lines largely similar from discipline to discipline, and with varying degrees of success. Disciplines are not then very usefully distinguished by
their methods. A literary man could well be interested in dating a piece
of literature. He will use methods and controls more commonly employed in other disciplines, comparison of documents, epigraphy, car-
bon 14. It all depends on the actual problem, though *this* problem, the
date of a literary document, came to his attention because he is a member of one of the literary disciplines. A discipline, as we said before, is
best defined from its object, its area of interest.

Yet saying this is not a way to dismiss the need for discriminating one
discipline from another. One does not discover intellectual objects by
"picking them up" casually. In the present state of knowledge, the
discrimination of an area of study is itself an exacting intellectual task
and one yielding great fruit. Each discipline must be aware with conscious precision how it brings its object into intellectual focus; for the
object of disciplined study is not found lying around, as it were, in
uncriticized common sense. It must be achieved, and it is ordinarily discerned by the efforts of experts. Literature is the object of the literary
disciplines. But literature is not simply a "given" of experience. The
determination of the literary object comprises much of the work of
literary study.

Or to take another example which, being hypothetical, may prove
malleable to our using it for purposes of illustration. Let us presume
— with no warrant that I am aware of — that the basic insight on
which the entire science of meteorology depends is that air is like
the ocean. Meteorologists on our assumption in making their decisions
as to whether a low pressure area will move from Arkansas to Ohio
would be reasoning according to laws that parallel those of hydrody-
namics. The science would then depend for its very existence on a firm
resistance being offered to the seductions of unexamined experience. For
"empty air" seems to be the most common conclusion which arises from
undisciplined perception, yet no one would make much of a meteorolo-

---

name. The actual university campus presents, the handiest avatar; but the academy
must include all serious scholarly communication: the journals, the reviews of opinion,
monographs, abstracts, conventions, and seminars, even, I suppose for the sake of
completeness we should add, private letters, snack bar conversations and gossip.

gist who went about arguing out his meteorological conclusions from a belief in "empty air." Meteorologists then became different from you and me. We may all be interested in the weather. (We are all subjected to it anyway.) But meteorologists, unlike commonsensical you and me, move about in an ocean of air, which is to say that they observe the object in question with a critical consciousness, the result of discipline. Now, it will not do for us to contend that it does not seem so very difficult to consider the air as ocean. Once you see it, it seems obvious. For the obviousness, of course, is the result of the same discipline having successfully communicated its discoveries to an undisciplined general public, who would otherwise still be beating the empty air.

Because we are able in a phenomenological overview like the present to see similarities among the disciplines this by no means makes them either less distinctively themselves or less usefully distinct. Disciplinary specialization is perhaps the greatest single factor in the technological successes of modern knowledge. Knowing with analytic sophistication the major insights which lie behind at least the major disciplines of the mind, will not substitute for close work within them. Air-as-ocean is a fine insight for anyone to have, but having it will not automatically produce knowledge of meteorological laws. It would be a cause of real regret if the rhetorical patterns adopted in this essay made it seem as though I were attempting to reduce the disciplines to one generalized lump. To argue that all knowledge is a human activity, similarly partial, questing and incomplete in all of even its disciplined forms, is not to argue that one of the necessary conditions of knowledge should not be a sense of achieving a certain finality of statement. The ultimate clarifying word is the aim of the one who seeks to know. It is the disciplines which have satisfied that cognitive appetite over and over, and they have done this by following the *divide et impera* injunction with great success.

I make these remarks here because in coming upon this last reason for theology's disciplinary need to consult constantly and reverently theological tradition, we have arrived at that specific element by which theology becomes itself. The revelation of the revealing God, which is the object the discipline of theology seeks to know, is therefore its specifying note, that by which theology becomes a discipline distinct from all others. I intend to use revelation only to reaffirm how necessary theology's use of tradition is to its enterprise. But it might legitimately be expected in an essay on "theology as an academic discipline" that I would try to define as precisely as I can how theology focuses its object, how, that is, it brings the revelation of God into intellectual range. But while this could have been a possible reading of my task, I have chosen to do something else. For two reasons: first, the polemical task bulked larger. It seemed to me that theology's need to defend her continued intellectual existence against those who do not love her was greater than examining, from the inside, her actual methods. These methods could conceivably become academic (in the Pickwickian sense) if the present disrepute of theology grows any more widespread. There will simply not be a sufficient number of talented theologians to make any difference. To defend theology's right to academic regard seemed crucial; and for this purpose, the present attempt to point out the similarities between it and other highly regarded disciplines recommended itself. Second, to distinguish with exactitude the object of any discipline is, as we have just seen, a task for the most precise disciplinary work. Only a theologian is equipped to define theology's object, to discriminate the actual from the apparent word of God.

Nevertheless, certain insights are possible even in the rather shoeless fashion in which we are viewing the academic scene and theology's place in it. I was at pains to point out that the knowledge theology seeks is faith-knowledge, that is, knowledge in and of faith. Our analysis at that point was essentially of the theological act proper to the theologian as knowing subject. I attempted to show that a discipline which seeks faith-knowledge must necessarily find some disciplinary expression of faith-fidelity in order to achieve its end. Thus the need of traditional thinking. What was perhaps only implicitly clear, however, in that analysis, was how strange an academic enterprise it is to seek faith-knowledge at all. For faith-knowledge implies that, in a very real sense, theology has no object. It is an exercise in what the phenomenologists call intersubjectivity. God uttering his word is what the theologian wants to know, which is to say, that what theology really wants to know is not an object, but another subject. It is as though the faithful husband of my parable not only wanted to know his wife and the fact of her fidelity, which, I trust we made clear, was a perfectly reasonable thing to want, but also wanted to write an encyclopedia on fidelity, a psychological tract on his and her fiidelity, an exhaustive analysis of the nuances of her character as evidenced in her letters and diaries and so forth. All of which could seem a very unreasonable thing to do indeed. One does not make a discipline out of personal knowledge of other persons.

The objection, put this way, seems very telling. Yet it is, I think, the same old horror of the pious at theology's presumption, here decked out in secular garb. We cannot allow it to detain us further than a brief pause for retort. Why *not* know persons with all the information and tools which can be brought to bear on them? Perhaps nothing is more important for us to know; and when the person in question is God, there is in a sense nothing else to know.

Our chief design, however, in pointing out this sharply specifying difference between theology and the rest of the academic disciplines was to reiterate and reinforce what we began by our analysis of faith-knowledge in the first place, that theology must be patient with tradition. The theologian, since the object of his discipline is the Revelation, the Word, of God, cannot as boldly experiment with fundamental insights and paradigmatic metaphors in his discipline as a researcher in another is free to do. He is forced to attend with great concentration to the presence of another person — God — speaking. Paradoxically, a subject is more really "objective," more insistently "other," "out there," than any *thing* else. For things can more easily be conceived as present only in our perception of them than persons will permit. The very perception of person is perception of a whole other universe of perception, so tantalizingly similar to our own, so agonizingly different.

To insist further on the special qualities of interpersonal knowledge might lend color to the charge so often laid against theology, that it is impervious to rationality, a matter of attending to "inner voices."[39] But this is a caricature. The theologian believes God speaks to him in a personal way and as an act of astonishing liberality, but only in and through the Church. It is God Incarnate in the living mystery of the Total Christ who faces the theologian and speaks. Because the present and speaking subject, God, is the object of his knowledge, the theologian, consequently, must anxiously scrutinize the faith of the Church. What the Church believes and teaches about God is the voice of God. The Christian theologian, therefore, who finds himself with *really* original ideas has cause for concern.

Yet having said all this we have merely sketched the difference be-

---

[39] I borrow the phrase and its derogatory nuances from James R. Newman who speaks in his Introduction to *What is Science?* (New York: Simon and Schuster, 1955) as follows: "I hope this book helps to a more balanced view both of science and human values. I hope it helps to counteract the malicious doctrines, flourishing again in this age of insecurity, which belittle science and reason, exhort men to consult their hearts instead of their heads, depreciate the lessons of experience and proclaim the higher truth emanating from inner voices," p. viii.

tween theology's object and those of other disciplines. We would not like to be understood as drawing a firm line between the intellectual practices of theology and those of other disciplines. No discipline is traditionless. Relativity, certainly one of the most revolutionary concepts of modern times, could scarcely have come about had Einstein been ignorant of the Maxwell-Lorenz equations which his own work superseded. Truth finding is, as we shall see at greater length later on, a social activity. We have been saying that the theologian must be faithful to the faith in order to be knowledgeable in the faith, that the Christian theologian, while he might hold his faith in a markedly idiosyncratic fashion, holds too that it did not come to him by his own efforts and that its features are none of his own choosing, and that, therefore, the Christian theologian is professionally bound to connect his own work with the traditional teaching of his discipline to a degree that, perhaps, does not obtain elsewhere.

But the theologian in his lesser *degree* remains free in exactly the same *sense* in which investigators in every other field are free. He is at liberty to push forward the bounds of knowledge, correct the mistakes and inadequacies of his predecessors, offer his own insights and formulations. The nature of the shared knowledge which constitutes a discipline does not change for those whose knowledge is in and of the faith. There is as much need for revision in theology as there is anywhere else. It must be more reverently applied, that is all.

At this point it becomes necessary to say a word about heresy. It should be stated that heresy is another fundamentally theological question to be treated like all such questions *within* the faith and not in an essay like this, which is no more than a narrowly-based prolegomenon to theology. I am not then, setting out to establish the theological status of heresy — by which I mean the moral status of the heretic, or the proper attitude of the faithful toward him. But it can be said that to the theologian as an academic man, by which I mean the theologian considered precisely as theologian rather than considered in his totality as believer, there is no such thing as heresy. There are only speculations about the faith which prove to be unhappy, uninformed, or corrigible by better speculations. Arius, to the theologian, helped to define one of the limits to correct thinking about faith in the Incarnation. He might even be legitimately honored as Newton is honored by Einsteinians, as Bohr is by researchers in mesons, as Luther is beginning to be by Catholic theologians. Pelagius, from a strictly academic point of view, contributed as genuinely, if not significantly, as did Augustine to our understanding of grace; Donatus was a valuable thinker in sacramental theology.

Theologians acting as such have always used heretics this way, defining their own ideas while using heretical teaching as a bench-mark to measure orthodoxy. Much as a Darwinian would give precise utterance to his own position by measuring it against a Lamarckian's. The difference is on that point of honor. Theological discourse ordinarily has had no stylistic provision for speaking well of theologians whose formulae have not been accepted by the Christian Church. A great deal could be made of this. Scientists and philosophers of science can be found who protest their shock at the lack of kindness and charity which they find prevalent among theologians. Their scandal often seems tinged with qualities of *scandulum pharasaicum* as it is invariably accompanied by praise for their own practice.[40] But the theologian refuses, customarily anyway, to speak well of his opponents not because he is a theologian, but because he is a member of the Church; and the Church following out her chief pastoral charge has not historically found it expedient to praise the erring. I say a great deal could be made of this and ecclesiastical officials as well as theologians should be aware of how much scandal in the modern, secularized academy this ancient practice does, in fact, occasion. Doubtless the rehabilitation of the reputations of heretics should be attended to immediately, wherever the facts will permit it. Otherwise the scholarly scandal remains in force. Nevertheless to fail to recognize that the Church's responsibility is more total (i.e., to the entire life of its members' faith, rather than merely to the rational understanding of their faith which is the theologian's proper preserve) is a failure in perception on the part of those university men who attack the entire theological enterprise on the grounds that the Church condemns heretics.[41]

We must not delay further on the question of heresy. It is not possible within the confines of this essay to treat all of the questions connected with theology's relation to authority with any great precision. They are numerous and difficult. Papal infallibility, and the authority of various

---

[40] For example, Bronowski in *Science and Human Values*, p. 88.

[41] On this question (or on so many others) Karl Rahner's thinking is highly illuminating, cf. *On Heresy* (Questiones Disputatae, No. 11), (New York: Herder and Herder, 1964). I would not venture to say that my remarks here are entirely in agreement with Father Rahner's precise and genuinely *theological* treatment of the matter. He seems more depressed by the lack of finality and clarity in modern thought than I find myself to be. But I do think we agree on the practical conclusions regarding heresy and heretics which the present state of intellectual affairs would indicate.

documents from the Holy See, conciliar statements and "irreformable" doctrine, the determinations of the universal *magisterium*, the relation of the Fathers and the opinions of older theologians to current theological discourse — these are not minor matters of methodology in theology. Indeed, one meets a bewildering variety of practice. Each theological thinker will bring his own temperament and predispositions to the question of authority. None will ignore it and remain a theologian and some will be more hidebound than others. None, however, will only repeat and collate "authorities" and remain a theologian. For the constant revision which we asserted was legitimate in theology is more than merely that. It is a disciplinary necessity as central in its sphere as consultation of tradition is in its. Revision is necessitated by the fact that theology's task is to bring understanding into mystery, where, by definition, conceptual understanding is only and always partial.

THEOLOGY AND MYSTERY

We have indicated that in the present state of knowledge-theory there is a great deal of confusion. Nevertheless a rough consensus seems to be coming into being which, since it cannot yet be so delimited that its contents are determined with precision and finality, must be described obliquely and metaphorically. The mind, by which I mean here rationality, namely the ability to conceptualize, abstract and submit to the test of internal consistency, is seen, in this emerging consensus I speak of, no longer as the apical point in man, as it has been for so long in the Western intellectual tradition of which Plato was the founding father: but simply as an instrument of man like hands or feet. In Bergson's thinking, for example, the mind becomes an almost biological extension of the human being, important, even if you want, essential, to human life, but not *the* core life in relation to which all other aspects of human life, emotions, physical growth, etc., are rind. If we must have an apical point in man, that for the modern can be nothing but his life itself. The appetite for totalities which the romantics bred in us out of their rejection of that ultimate Platonism, the rationalism of the eighteenth century, is insatiable. Nothing partial will satisfy it and certainly not the merely conceptualizing mind. There is no "highest" part of man, there is no "realist" part. All parts are servants. Everything must attend on living, ineffable man himself.

Once one is determined to use his intellect to bring himself to a greater mastery of the concrete, he is left in an unenviable noetic position. For the cognitive movement is always first one out *from* unanalyzed experience, the concrete, into pattern and abstraction, then, secondly, one back *into* experience. At the end of this second moment within the process of cognition the knower inevitably finds that the patterned analysis he has constructed, doubtless after much effort and pain, is inadequate, partial, in desperate need of extension, qualification, or discard. This leaves the modern thinker with roughly three options. He can forget the post-Romantic ideal of cognitively dominating concrete experience. This is what, by and large, and often merely for purposes of method (though unsophisticated practitioners confuse method and substance frequently), the physical sciences have choosen to do. With practical ends in view they have stayed within the cozy fencing of rationalism and have enjoyed a high degree of success. Not only that, but their success is in function of their cognitive conservatism. For, by agreeing to work within what are roughly the same few frameworks, scientists are enabled very exhaustively to explore nature.[42]

The second option is to refuse to leave the concrete. Actually this is an oversimplification of the cognitive strategy I have in mind. I phrase it this way for purposes of schematic clarity. But what I am referring to is the methodological preference of poets and artists. W. B. Yeats in a famous letter which, since it was written six days before his death, is often taken as a kind of final testament and summary of his methods, puts the whole business very eloquently.

> I know for certain that my time will not be long. I have put away everything that can be put away that I may speak what I have to speak and I find my expression is part of 'Study.'
> In two of three weeks — I am now idle that I may rest after writing much verse — I will begin to write my most fundamental thoughts and the arrangement of thought which I am convinced will complete my studies. I am happy and I think full of an energy I had despaired of. It seems to me that I have found what I wanted. When I try to put all into a phrase I say: 'Man can embody truth but he cannot know it.' I must embody it in the completion of my life. The abstract is not life and everywhere drags out its contradictions. You can refute Hegel but not the Saint or the Song of Sixpence.[43]

Note that the insight of the last few sentences is the result of "study."

[42] Cf. Mr. Kuhn's telling treatment of this matter in the *Structure of Scientific Revolutions*, the last chapter, "Progress through Revolutions," pp. 159–172 *passim*.
[43] Quoted in Richard Ellman's biography, *Yeats: The Man and the Masks* (New York: E. P. Dutton and Co., 1948), p. 285, paperback.

This seeming rejection of cognition — "man cannot *know* truth" — is nevertheless a "fundamental *thought* and the arrangement of *thought*." There is to be pattern here, the result of study and thought, but a pattern in and of the concrete. Perhaps we can most quickly elucidate this second option by an example. Yeats is describing that special use of metaphorical thinking which has come to be referred to as symbolic, adopting the name originally from the practice and literary theory of the symbolist poets.

> The paired butterflies are already yellow with August
> Over the grass in the West garden;
> They hurt me. I grow older.

Here we have three lines from Ezra Pound's poem "The River Merchant's Wife." The passage is a patterned selection from the manifold of experience. Thus, this sum of images, the yellow paired butterflies, August, the grass, the West Garden, hurt and growing old, all form a constellation whose meaning is definite enough. They certainly do not sum up to a meaning that could be paraphrased as "Life is just a bowl of cherries." The area of experience they indicate is ordinarily named in such words as "nostalgia," "loneliness," "abandonment," or that most esthetic of emotions, "self-pity." Furthermore we can be even more precise. Growing old stands together with "already yellow," "August," "*West* garden" (the one in the direction of sunset and consequently of the elder state of things). The paired butterflies can be assumed not merely to be associated with "hurt" but perhaps in some measure causing it — out of an envious perception on the part of the lonely woman of contrast between her state and theirs. The grass they fly over seems to function chiefly as a signal of the piece's style by insisting on the concreteness of this diction in the same way that blazer, straw hat and cane signal that the dancer is about to perform a soft shoe not a flamenco.

Yet while this is all very precise it is not sufficiently so to satisfy our appetite for precision. Truth "embodied" in the concrete symbol is not, as Yeats said, "known," in the sense that one possesses it and controls it. Paired yellow butterflies, presented as such, do not change the fact that butterflies do not necessarily say sorrow and could, as the butterfly in Robert Frost's poem "A Tuft of Flowers" say the hope that survives sorrow. And though one might legitimately wither with literary scorn the simpleton who read Pound's butterflies as signifying hope or gaiety, or something equally inappropriate to his intention, at the same time one would have to recognize that the error is not totally indefensible.

It can be attributed to inherent deficiencies in the cognitive strategies of symbolist discourse. The concrete presented in its concreteness cannot be so controlled that its cognitive yields are precisely limited. The protest, "But butterflies always make *me* happy," is certainly inappropriate, but also irrefutable. Furthermore the concrete, patterned though it be in this kind of discourse, is not so patterned that the full intention of the speaker is either unambiguously clear or, always, immediately clear. The meaning we have assigned to the garden being a *West* garden seems sound enough on reflection; but it does need reflection, that is, it does not insist on itself being recognized on first hearing. Consequently, the suspicion that "West equals old" is to be attributed more to the ingenuity of the critical reader than either to the intention of the writer or necessarily to the inherent intention of the piece, is one that arises and persists in contentious minds with some color of justification.

Symbolist communication in and of the concrete must try to make the concrete meaningful. It does this by patterning images in the way we have seen. It also does it often enough by flatly declaring a limited meaning in a fairly arbitrary manner. In the same way that the mathematician says "let x equal y," Ezra Pound in the phrase "yellow with August" says, "let yellow be the result of August and reinforce the meaning which August conveys in this concrete pattern of imagery." For, although I am innocent of any knowledge of lepidoptera I would be surprised to find that the color of butterflies is a phenomenon that changes with the month.

The third option for thinkers who are determined to know concrete reality is to follow the movement of thought from life to idea and back again in a process that refuses to hope for finality. This is what, for the most part, is the procedure favored by the disciplines called "humanistic." There are, of course, literary critics, art theoreticians, historians, and philosophers who are pattern mongerers and systematizers. They would, if they could, impose a finality of famework on their disciplines much on the model of the physical sciences. "Sciolists all, pickpockets and opinionated bitches,"[44] as Yeats calls such thinkers, they ambition an amplitude to their conceptions which would make these everlastingly irreformable. Future generations of thinkers would need only to recapture *their* meaning and extend *their* insights. Enough has been said to present my reasons for rejecting such a program. The impossibility of main-

[44] From "The Death of Cuchulain," in *Collected Plays of W. B. Yeats* (London: Macmillan, 1952), p. 694.

taining even largely conceived frameworks and paradigms in the physical sciences where they can be best maintained, has been sufficiently indicated to make evident the foolhardiness of attempting to erect such permanent conceptual structures in the humanities. The material of the humanistic disciplines will not brook abstraction and pattern with anything like the same degree of acquiescence as the material of physics and chemistry. For the material of the humanistic disciplines is too close to the personal order of being; and consequently it presents to the thinker who seeks to control it an insistent resistance to being patterned, as persons *will* insist on being understood on their own terms rather than on those chosen for them by others.

Philosophers, social scientists, litterateurs, and historians for the most part, resign themselves to being consumers of ideas. A mental pattern which seems to hold great promise and to establish a measure of control over an extensive area of experience, quickly becomes too narrow to contain this or that new event of the various human history, or is seen to have forgotten this or that quite common manifestation of the fecundity of human ingenuity, or is found on reflection to be trite, inappropriate, or obsolete. It is impossible to adopt a few frameworks and explore them exhaustively because their inadequacy so quickly becomes evident on this level of unabstracted experience. Here voices clamor contentiously for answers which they will not attend to in any case, being too anxious to represent their own point of view. The harried scholar in the humanities who listens at all is surrounded by din. If he reads the journals he will soon find little leisure for exhaustive exploration of his own insights. On the other hand a resolute humanistic thinker who does pursue the implications of a "system" despite his colleagues' mockeries and his own misgivings, may win great regard but a regard more often accorded his courage than his conclusions. Few men have disciples; fewer have disciples who prove faithful over many years; fewer still have disciples who actually extend the insights of the master without adulterating them. Aristotelianism, Platonism, Thomism, these are sectarian tags which label some very diverse thinkers. A Hegel or a Toynbee win a measure of respectful attention, but few devotees.

Researchers in those areas which are of interest to the humanistic disciplines continue to accept and discard ideas with bewildering rapidity. For the reasons adumbrated above, namely that the mere patterning of concretions remains too cognitively dissatisfying, the methods of the poets and artists remain more the material of the humanities rather than being adopted as their cognitive methods as well. Patterning concretions in the manner of the symbolist poets is an excellent method for highlighting and focusing experience. It selects from the manifold of experience and presents its selection with great immediacy and point. This is an important first step to achieving that control over experience which is the end of the cognitive drive, but it is only a *first* step. Even vivid presentation does not of itself make the area presented more subservient to our will. It may result in our recognizing ways to repeat, limit, manipulate, transfer this vividly presented experience into other contexts of our own choosing. Our recognition may be a direct result of the vividness of the presentation, but no mere presentation no matter how successfully vivid, contains the recognition of the means to control in itself. To achieve control one must abstract. "The Saint and Song of Sixpence" can adjust our view of things, offered a clarifying intensity of vision in which ways to control come into focus. But controls must always be translated into prescription for true controls will be handled by a very diverse selection of operators. Prometheus needed not only to bring fire from heaven, but to teach many unheroic types the proper methods of kindling it at will. The language of prescription will always be abstract, for an abstract vocabulary is the only one which has a chance of getting through the idiosyncratic thickets which guard the passage from everyman's ear to his brain. Interpretation, an inevitability, has less chance to obscure intention when the language is that of abstract concept.

Between these two poles, the resistance his material offers to abstraction, and the cognitive imprecision of concretion, the scholar of the humanities makes his sinuous way. The movement of his mind is systaltic and ceaseless. He becomes a conspicuous consumer of concepts and formulations and the good order of this discipline is minimal. In comparison with the relative stability of the enumerating disciplines the state of affairs in any of the humanities can be fairly characterized as chaotic. And with the failure to establish the epistemological model of rationalism, there has come to be a kind of contentment with confusion in the humanities. Once the mind is no longer seen as essentially passive to the intelligibility of things, to "objective truth," but rather actively cooperating in that symbiosis of subject and object which I offered previously as an expression more nearly approximating the postrationalistic epistemological models, the expectation of final comprehension recedes. Mystery returns to serious consideration.

For the rationalists "mystery" meant merely the unknown. It named the extraterrestrial, the divine order of being in the thinking of theistic rationalists. Their expectation was that, given sufficient time and will, all directly experienced reality could be definitively uttered. Therefore the truths revealed by the revealing God, as these could only exist trans-experientially, were exempted from the necessity of being comprehensively understood and were categorized as "mystery." With the growth of secular rationalism during the Enlightenment, "mystery" was seen to be only a clerical stratagem by which inquiry could be choked off with taboo. But theists and secularists agreed that mystery was the unknown; the name marked a failure in the cognitive enterprise. This is no longer quite true. The word retains much of its negative flavor especially in the vocabulary of those thinkers who hanker still for the sharp-edged epistemologies of rationalism. But there is a positive side to the concept which grows in importance, in function, I think, of the growth of that consensus concerning the nature of knowledge we glanced at at the beginning of this section.

When the epistemological criticisms of the rationalists' model of knowledge first began to have their effect in the intellectual world. The effects were, as could be anticipated from such a radical departure, very various ranging from bright optimism to gray fear. Shelley, seeing that man makes the forms of his own understanding, hailed the poets as "the unacknowledged legislators of the world," whereas Arnold and Eliot could see in poetic conceptions no more than ineffectual fragments. The modern mind is keenly aware of the massive importance of subjectivity in all knowledge; and its reaction to this awareness has been both positive and negative. But perhaps it is true to say that a pessimistic reaction characterized the nineteenth century and has begun to give way to more hopeful views. Recognizing the subjectivity of knowledge seemed at first destructive of all security, all certainty. Man's intellect, ruthlessly criticizing its own productions was:

> Ravening, raging and up-rooting that he may come
> Into the desolation of reality.[45]

But it is the same poet who later on commemorates, in no unambiguous way, but certainly out of no final despair, the fact that all lofty concept and intellectual aspirations "start/In the foul rag-and-bone shop of the heart."[46]

[45] Yeats, "Meru," *Collected Poems* (New York: Macmillan, 1957), p. 287.
[46] Yeats, "The Circus Animals' Desertion," *Collected Poems*, p. 336.

No epistemology which ignores the break with the rationalistic model, which seeks to dismiss the subjectivity of knowing, can win much support today. "Objective truth" awaiting the discovery of industrious research and rigorous logic no longer recommends itself as a possible goal. The rationalistic interpretation of knowledge has led to its own defeat because it insisted that its purpose was to control what it had finally to recognize controls it — the life of the knowing subject. One modern position which has emerged from the defeat of rationalism sees knowledge as mere instrument, a tool man used to extend the scope of his power. This position (by it I mean to embrace the whole variety of pragmatic theories) continues the Promethean aspirations of rationalism and signals its modernity primarily by emphasizing the arbitrariness, the "discardibility" of all knowledge.

Often the pragmatists argue their theory by showing how much it is "on the side of life" in its refusal to allow man to fetter himself in his own conceptual chains. But to other modern thinkers the knowledge theory of the pragmatists insufficiently recognizes the fundamental difference between rationalism and what has come to take its place. The drive to know, as this second school sees it, remains in pragmatism radically unchanged from what rationalism claimed it was, despite the pragmatists emphasis on the instrumentality of concepts. For in its pure manifestation knowing would still accomplish nothing less than the total subjugation of reality. Yet, what must be admitted according to these other thinkers is that the subjugation of reality is an overambitious and "anti-life" goal in itself. Reality, or the more fashionable term, "existence," can never be uttered in controlling concepts, but only indicated, gestured at and, of course, lived. Knowledge to this second criteriological school appears, in the theories of the pragmatists, to be the same presumptuous, even vulgar assault on life which it was under rationalism.

The Keatsian sigh for a "life of sensation without thought," the Romantic celebration of the primitive, the instinctual and the childish, the attack of the aesthetically-minded on the utilitarians, the scientists, industrialists, and politicians, phenomenological and existentialistic theories and attitudes — these characteristic features of modern intellectual life, all belong to this second interpretation of the meaning of the defeat of rationalism. Positively, the proponents of this second position seem to emphasize that aspect of modern epistemology we have previously named as a symbiosis between knowing man and the nature from which he emerges.

It has been my contention that the rejection of theology's claim for place in the academic task on epistemological grounds is ordinarily based on an exploded rationalistic epistemology. Since this is so, I have used any descriptions of the thought process as that is understood by nonrationalistic thinkers without bothering until now to disinglish between them. Thus I have spoken of thought, sometimes as an instrument for control of nature, sometimes as a means of achieving an experienced union with nature, although I am aware that these two descriptions have their separate origins in quite antithetical modern schools. I have done this because I am convinced that a reconciliation between these divergent schools is possible. (Let us for convenience name them from now on the "Promethean" and the "mystical.") I suggest that the point of reconciliation is in the concept of mystery, positively defined.

If mystery is seen not merely as a failure in knowledge, a verbal shrug of nescience, it can offer, I think, an area where Promethean and mystic can agree. The pragmatic thinker, no less, than his mystical counterpart, is aware of the pretensiousness of rationalism. Both are aware that no "nomological net" can snare the real, at least for good. In this mutual awareness is their point of agreement. They really agree, then though the word may offend some members of the Promethean school, that cognition seeks always to explore "mystery" which term we can define as reality experienced suprarationally, with more than rational faculties, not less.

Before that agreement the seemingly deep divisions in the modern intellectual world shrink, it seems to me, into mere sectarian quibbles. The utilitarian with all his Promethean aspirations is not the insensitive vulgarian that mystical thinkers would have him appear, but a courageous and humble searcher of the mysteries of the universe whose rejection of easy certainties constitutes his own act of reverence to the inexhaustible richness of existence. On the other hand, the mystic, with all his apparent inertia, is rapt by the same central vision as the pragmatist who mocks him: the incomprehensibility of experience. The real difference between these two schools is one of temperament, not of substance. Set two representatives of these two modern views side by side on the seashore: one will be stilled to a quiet inner state in which all the vastness of wind, wave, and beach is held in a single, wordless apprehension of totality; the other will be galvanized into a fury of mental activity, temperature of the water? geological formation of the beach? real estate possibilities? origins of the shells and stones in the sand? etc. Both the mystical inner silence and the restless demand for information have their origin, however, in the same source, namely, that especially modern intellectual position we have been calling the rejection of rationalism. Or put more positively, the origin of both mystical and pragmatic views can be traced to that perception, fundamental to modern thought, that experience always transcends whatever can be said about it, which is another way of saying that man lives surrounded by mystery.

The traditional thinker often held that man lived in an envelope of mystery but, unlike the modern, he attributed this to powers and forces which he defined as lying beyond his experience. The world at his nerve-ends might prove ineffable but only inasmuch as it was subject to extraterrestrial manipulation. Left alone, it would, eventually anyway, be totally revealed to his industrious understanding. The modern antirationalistic thinker has, through an epistemological analysis of his own act of understanding, recognized that mystery pervades his cognitive life. Experience itself, not extraterrestrial meddling, is sufficient cause for the perception of mystery. Or, to use even more explicitly religious terminology, the minimal enabling condition for genuine knowledge is a perception of the sacred.[47]

I have tried to show that mystery has descended from the sky and walks the earth as the companion of man's daily experience. This is a reading of the meaning of the last century or two of man's understanding of his own thinking. I am not confident that I have been able so to state this position that it will persuade anyone predisposed to reject religious language. Nevertheless, I would hope I have been able at least to persuade the religious-minded, those we have been calling "mystics" and whose mind-set is characterized by a proclivity for hieratic language and an intention to achieve an experienced union with reality, that their polemic against utilitarian and Promethean thinkers is sterile. The Promethean may lack reverence and an aesthetically satisfying humility;

---

[47] It should be evident to anyone acquainted with it, that I have been influenced in my thinking here by Rudolf Otto's *The Idea of the Holy* (New York: Galaxy Books, Oxford University Press, 1958). My own thinking runs beyond Otto's, however, since I am less reluctant than he to extend the area of the holy. I contend, perhaps influenced by my reading of Romantic Literature, that all things are holy and that no one can claim genuinely to perceive anything unless he also perceives it numinously. Gabriel Marcel's distinction between "mystery" and "problem" makes interesting reading on this point. Cf. *The Philosophy of Existence*. trans. Manya Harari (London, 1948), the first chapter, "On the Ontological Mystery," pp. 1–30.

but his readiness to change his mind and his *formulae* is recognition in action that experience remains ineffable. He too perceives the sacred, but prefers not to call it such.

For this reason I think an apology for religious thinking which bases itself on a polemic against utilitarian thinking is beside the point at least epistemologically speaking. Even the irenic John Henry Newman lapses into a slanging of the utilitarians, and it often seems to constitute the entire substance of the *apologiae* of Chesterton and Belloc and the highly articulate, frequently very wise school, which derives from them: Ronald Knox, C. S. Lewis, Charles Williams, Owen Barfield, etc. Still one can understand the impatience of the religious apologists, for it must be considered strange that while the whole world of man's experience has become suffused in mystery, there is so little regard paid to the one discipline which enjoys a tradition of dealing with mystery, and has attempted to give what utterance it can to the ineffable. The discipline of theology has until now proved almost useless for the modern inquirer despite that fact that theology's traditional task can be said to have become in the modern age of knowledge the task of every discipline.

I have already strongly implied that I think it a mistake — strategic, if not indeed substantive — to attribute the neglect of theology to the pretentions of utilitarianism. Let me state that position now with emphatic explicitness. Theology's neglect in the modern antirationalist age is not to be attributed exclusively to the residue of rationalism in science, technology and the other utilitarian disciplines of the mind. But rather theology's neglect at least as often must be charged to the residue of rationalism in theology itself.

Throughout the ages of the rationalistic tradition it was theology's task resolutely to rebuke the pretentions of that tradition by continually reminding the human mind that, since the heart of reality was the ineffable God, the final, clarifying word would always elude it. Now that a hope of ultimate clarity is no part of anyone's cognitive expectation, Western theology is often found mindlessly reiterating dead *formulae* as though these had uniquely and ultimately enunciated reality.

The situation is ironic and the irony is tragic. The fidelity which the theologian owes to the tradition of theological thought and formulation is, as we developed at length, real and operative; but, if it so inhibits his speculation that he is unable to revolutionize the *formulae* of his discipline with the same qualified confidence that any thinker brings to the task of proposing his own formulations, then not only is his own thought and that of his discipline moribund, but such servile fidelity flatly contradicts the primary aim of the discipline itself, namely, to elucidate to the limit of possibility the fecund elusiveness of mystery. For to fulfill that aim, it is necessary ceaselessly to produce new formulations. The "third cognitive option" which we saw at the beginning of this section is the only one open to the theologian. A tireless revision of concept and language is necessarily imposed on him, for as a theologian he has taken as his province the elucidation of experience as mystery.

Theological Verification

At this point we are ready to consider the second half of the epistemological question which was first placed earlier. I have argued that the result of the speculations concerning the nature of knowledge during the last two hundred years has been to emphasize very strongly that knowledge arises from a commitment on the part of the knowing subject to the truth, the usefulness or, perhaps, merely the elegance, of his theory. That is to say, there is no very precise answer available to the first epistemological enquiry, "How do we know?" except to say that knowledge arises when the knower finds himself possessed of an idea or insight and is prepared to assent to it. There is then no knowledge which is not in some measure an act of faith on the part of the knower. Since there is no very great cognitive security to be found in the analysis begun with the first question "How do we know?," epistemological speculation hastens to ask the second question concerning the verification of knowledge, namely, "How do we know that we know?"

The question of verification is one which it seems the physical sciences have managed to answer with wonderful confidence and clarity. A theory is verified when it has predicted results and demonstrated the accuracy of its predictions empirically. The test of scientific thinking is the experiment. This analysis of scientific procedure is at least as old as Bacon's *Novum Organum*, but cannot be any longer maintained than his equally erroneous contention that science characteristically develops its theories by induction. As we have seen, the strength of the scientific disciplines is to be attributed much more to their willingness to abstract from concrete experience in pursuit of the certainties of generalizations than to any highly developed appetite for "given facts." From the work of Kuhn, Frank, Sellars, Scriven, among others[48] it is becoming clear that

[48] Cf. *Structure of Scientific Revolutions,* Wilfrid Sellars, "Empiricism and the

the ability to predict laboratory results does not assure the truth of a scientific theory, much less its acceptance. The general tenor of Kuhn's argument is that even when a theory has ceased to be useful or even is seen to be quite mistaken in several large sectors of the areas of experience it seeks to explain, it will often continue to win a wide assent in the community of scientists.

The relationship between a theory's ability to predict results, and its acceptance by the members of a discipline as validated, is a complex one which is inadequately understood in the commonsense understanding that predicted results "demonstrate" the truth of the theory. Because both give excellent predictions, both discrete and continuous theories of electromagnetic energy flourish side by side. Einstein's general theory of relativity began to find wide acceptance after it had predicted the variation in the perihelion of Mercury, a single experiment, rarely repeatable. This acceptance took place even though most of the theory's central ideas seemed quite untestable at the time. Indeed, many of the hypotheses of general relativity stand without empirical verification of any kind even today, and yet provide the conceptual framework for a vast amount of physical investigations. The Copenhagen model of the basic structures of matter is incompatible in certain important particulars with that implied in Schrödinger's equations, but both are successfully used by researchers.

Perhaps we can best illustrate the complexity of the relation in scientific thinking between a theory's ability to yield predicted results and its acceptance as a "verified" hypothesis by turning to psychology. We lose something of the precision and exactitude available in theories arising out of the strictly physical sciences, but, since the instances do not demand the same technical proficiency as an examination of physics, we may gain fuller clarity.

A patient subject to hallucinations could conceivably be cured by a Freudian, an Adlerian, a Jungian, an "objectivist," or by a theoretical agnostic like Carl Rogers. All would have results to show from procedures arising from thoroughly different hypotheses. As we know from

---

Philosophy of Mind," esp. sections 32–44 in *Minnesota Studies in the Philosophy of Science*, vol. I (Minneapolis, 1956), p. 253 ff. Michael Scriven in an essay in the same volume entitled "A Possible Distinction between Traditional Scientific Disciplines and the Study of Human Behavior," develops the absence of successful predictability in behavioristic studies as one of the possible marks of distinction. Philipp G. Frank, "The Variety of Reasons for the Acceptance of Scientific Theories," in *The Validation of Scientific Theories* (New York: Collier Books, 1961), p. 13 ff.

the testimony of their inventors, psychological theories were often formed on little empirical evidence. Freud seems to have based much of his theory on Josef Breuer's experience in curing a young girl of her paralysis, and Jung's patient who had a dream in 1906 of an ancient Mithraic ritual seems to have convinced him of the existence of a collective unconsciousness.[49] Yet these theories, despite their presentation on such slim evidence, have proved useful and have won very wide acceptance. We are ready, I think, at least in psychological matters, to admit that experience is mystery before which all theory is a mere mental gesture inadequate to encompass the whole. The human fact — an hallucinating patient in our example — is simply larger than what the various psychologists can say about him. All might manage to be instruments of his regaining health. All might be right in their explanation; or none might be. What we probably cannot admit is that anyone of them is exclusively and comprehensively right.

The state of psychological knowledge is not unique. It is merely easier to see there what is the general state of scientific knowledge. A scientific theory in physics and chemistry does not become verified in the sense that it is seen to state "the truth" apodictically simply because it manages to predict results. There have been too many theories which, although they yielded a large harvest of predictions, have been subsequently discarded in the course of the history of science, for us to maintain any longer that simple Baconian view. The situation we spoke of in the previous section obtains in science as well as elsewhere: concrete experience always resists ultimate formulation in abstract categories. The world of fact, too, is mystery.

What, then, is the nature of verification? Acceptance of a hypothesis within the community of scholars one is addressing, constitutes the establishment of that hypothesis as valid. Predicted laboratory results are a customary means of moving the scientific community to accept an hypothesis. They operate, not as a "demonstration" in the sense that they reveal without the possibility of further argument the truth of the hypothesis they were designed to support; rather they operate much in the way that an elegant phrase or a moving gesture does for the public

[49] Cf. A. A. Brill's introduction to *The Basic Writings of Sigmund Freud* (New York: Modern Library, 1938), p. 7, also Freud, "On the History of the Psycho-Analytic Movement" in the *Complete Works* (London: Hogarth. 1957), Vol. 14, pp. 8–9. For Jung see "The Concept of Collective Unconscious," in *The Collected Works of C. J. Jung*, trans. R. F. C. Hull (New York: Bollingen Series XX, 1959), Vol. IX, pp. 42–53.

speaker. They are the rhetorical stratagems most highly, though not exclusively, valued within scientific discourse. Predicted laboratory results are highly persuasive, that is their value. Much like the prestidigitator's, or the pitchman's ritual phrase "I tell ya what I'm gonna do!" they stun and astonish the mind into acquiesence. They are the means to verification in that they move the community of scientists to accept the theory they support; and *acceptance is all the verification a theory needs, wants, or can find.*

This may seem a startling conclusion to some, since the conviction that a final, conceptually expressed clarity can be achieved by the questing human mind has so long undergirded the Western intellectual tradition. But I do not think it will greatly surprise anyone whose intellectual interests have led him to reflect upon the epistemological investigations of the past two centuries. No matter how variously the conviction is expressed, the modern epistemological position is fundamentally different from that of the tradition. It sees, as we have been attempting to elucidate for some pages now, all conceptualization as an abstraction, that is a reduction of the plenitude of concrete experience and which is, consequently, necessarily incapable of uttering experience fully or accurately. Since this is so, mystery, at least in the sense of ineffability, is the end of all human intellectual activity. Whether one is moved by this state of affairs to *o altitudo* or nailing-biting or both, may be in function of one's temperament, training, or state of health; but if one is faithful to his intellectual drive, the end of one intellectual quest is always the beginning of another. It follows from all this that the form of truth is a process; a development, an evolution, perhaps, but always, at least, a movement. If no concept can be total as the experience out of which it arises is total, then it must be succeeded by a corrective concept. Dialectic, then, is the shape of living knowledge.

This is why the university or academy is such a crucial feature of modern intellectual work. The best thinkers, in the sense of the most valuable to the continuing intellectual process, are almost always university men who are engaged in the restless scrimmage of ideas which is the condition of academic life. Earlier models of intellectual work could offer a basis for celebrating retirement. Contemplative isolation was the customary ideal of the intellectual, since there, undisturbed by his colleague's questionings, the thinker could forge theory into truth, or that seeming of truth which is the comprehensive "system." This is no longer a defensible ideal, in my opinion.

Though I am not contending that contemplative isolation, where the mind reflecting upon its own experience is enabled to generate insight, is a dispensible part of the intellectual process, I do contend that the entire process is speeded up, the moment of contemplative isolation is fleeting, and that the agent of this acceleration is the university. The process, because it takes place in the university and under the aegis of modern epistemological speculation, has been much more thoroughly and consciously "socialized."

It seems to me to work this way: a thinker by contemplative reflection on his own experience achieves a sense of pattern, an "idea" that is, a perception of structure, order, or direction in that experience. He wrestles to articulate this perception and submits it to the judgment of his intellectual peers. At this point (which is rather more quickly reached than in the pre-epistemological era, because the thinker in question is less disposed to examine exhaustively all the implications of his pattern, being aware that no matter how exhaustively he does so, he cannot establish his pattern as the eternal utterance of even his own experience of the concrete) dialectic begins. Analyses of the pattern's consistency are offered, objections are raised, alternatives proposed. The state of affairs at this point in the intellectual process is very much like a political debate. And this is not in itself surprising since a practical issue of importance to many people is exactly what is being debated. Whether the proposed pattern of understanding is going to prove a rich source of further insight and control of experienced reality, or not, is a matter of practical, social concern; for if the consensus is that it will, the last stage of verification as that process is proper to the formal academy is reached. A number of investigators decide to adopt this pattern as the frame of their own research. The original insight becomes now the foundation of disciplined work, the ground of a science, as such.

With acceptance within the academy established, the research can be conducted in that relative peace which Mr. Kuhn describes as the state of "normal science." It is in this period too that acceptance begins to extend itself outside the bounds of the formal academy. The original insight is communicated ever more widely and finds a more extensive acceptance. It becomes more verified, "truer," as it serves as the frame for more and more peoples' understanding of their own experience. The ultimate verification of the theory of the electron can be said to be the steady profit realized in General Electric stocks.

The history of scientific acceptance or verification is exactly paralleled in theological verification. A theologian perceives what he thinks is a new and useful insight into the nature of the mysterious experience of faith. Ordinarily, I suppose, this insight is generated by his personal experience of belief; but in the same way that the scholarly profession of the scientist or other intellectual researcher acts to make him a disciplined thinker, the theologian, schooled by his discipline and faithful to its traditional formulations with that extraordinary fidelity which we saw must characterize him, strives to articulate this new insight in terms which make it expressive of not only his personal experience of faith, but much more, of that of the Church.[50] He submits his formula in the first instance to his fellow theologians and, granted it finds acceptance among them, to the whole community of the Church. When a theologian's speculations become part of the Church's understanding of its faith in Christ, by say, conciliar definition, or, even more, by inclusion in the ordinary teaching of the Church — catechisms, parochial sermons, etc., then these speculations have reached the final state of verification, paralleling the seal set upon the existence of the electron by the existence of R.C.A. and Westinghouse.

We have witnessed recently the entire process from insight to common teaching completed within a relatively few years. The theological speculations of Karl Rahner, Henri de Lubac and Yves Congar to cite a few, first came to light, for the most part, after World War II. Their publications were ordinarily greeted with the consternation and disturbance which ripples through any scholarly community when its customary assumptions are questioned. But the consistency and persuasiveness of their books won them an ever-widening hearing among theologians, which culminated in many of their formulations being adopted in the decrees of the Second Vatican Council. It is as a result of that acceleration in development which, as we said before, is a modern feature of all intellectual work, that we are able to see the pattern of theological verification so succinctly and clearly today. St. Thomas' Aristotelian synthesis of Christian faith, for example, did not find place in the ordinary teaching of the Church until the Fifth Lateran Council, years after his death, and it was not until Trent more than two centuries after he died that his structures became

---

[50] The attempt the theologian makes to render his personal insight an expression of the Church's Faith is paralleled by the description Alfred Schutz gives of the social scientist transforming his personal insight into a disciplinary framework. Cf. *Collected Papers* (The Hague: Martinas Nijhoff, 1962), Vol. I, p. 63.

fully established as the ordinary expressions of orthodoxy. But the accelerated pace of recent theological development allows us to see the entire process of verification from start to finish, and to see that its movement parallels the process of verification in all other branches of intellectual activity.

With this much said our defense of theology's right to academic status is finished. In the matter of verification, too, the intellectual practices of theologians differ in nothing essential from those of the most highly regarded disciplines. If a resolute positivist wishes to argue for the exclusive intellectual cogency of empirical demonstration which seemingly is such a salient feature of the verification of physical theories, he will need to fault all of the humanities and most of the social sciences for not supporting their insights with laboratory results. Furthermore he will need to explain with great precision how predicted results do, in fact, verify by their own demonstrative power alone, what prove to be corrigible theories. He will, finally, need to defend the naïvete of his epistemology: for he is still ignoring the voluntary and credal dimension of all thought in the hope of finding the now untenable model of pure rationalism defensible.

But we have offered more than a merely negative defense of theology's practices and methods. In drawing parallels between theology's concept of its intellectual task and those of other disciplines we have asserted that, far from suffering from unique cognitive deficiencies because of its commitment to faith, theology is the oldest discipline in intellectual history to realize the nature of all human cognitive activity as that has been revealed in epistemological analysis. Theology, in asserting its need to ground its insights in a prior commitment of faith, and in its contention that all its formulations can never be more than gestures at the ineffability of the mysteries it seeks to utter, anticipated the findings of nearly two centuries of rational analysis of the cognitive process which have permanently humbled the pretensions of rationalism. It would, of course, be quite historically inaccurate to claim that theologians have always been sophisticated modern epistemologists, self-consciously aware of the structure of insight and verification, as we have outlined it here. It was precisely during the centuries when theology queened it at the universities that the rationalistic model of understanding found its clearest articulation. And when, during the Enlightenment especially, the pretensions of rationalism became really excessive, the customary response of theology was to tend in the direction of abandoning its own commitment to credal thinking for an even more assertive rationalism than that which confronted it.[51] Until the mid-nineteenth century Catholic theology, at least, appeared committed totally to the sterilities and consequent irrelevance of rationalism. Some of the preparatory schemata for the First Vatican Council and many of the subsequent theological clarifications and developments of its decrees seem to be rooted in the quite heterodox position that faith is deducible from the rational analysis of concepts, supported only by a logical consistency.[52] Nevertheless, theology, because it has always been the "science of faith," has operated within precisely those structures of understanding which we see now are the only ones available to human cognition. Whatever reason one might justly use to reject the theological enterprise for himself or others, he cannot legitimately accuse it of being no true discipline of the mind because of its dependence on faith and its admission of mystery. It has been to render that accusation, the most common justification for disregarding theology, invalid, that this essay has been written.

Two final points. In this postrationalistic age where it is clear that, as Herbert Gold remarks, "experience is the walls of our room," it is pointless to reach beyond experience for meanings and values. Premodern thinkers, convinced that their conceptualizations could penetrate to an eternal, or at least a transtemporal order of reality, looked for verticalities which thrust quite out of sight. A hierarchy of worth and significance, fixed forever in some empyrean available only to the mind, was the aim of the true intellectual for, having achieved that, he possessed a secure way to measure and judge the passing show of

---

[51] We have already commemorated the efforts in this direction of Malebranche and the Occasionalistic theologians (p. 40). To prove that this tendency was not confined to Catholic Europe, it is perhaps well to recall that a theological demonstration founded on rationalistic grounds is the aim and method of the famous *Analogy* of Bishop Butler of England.

[52] The proof of God's existence by unaided reason as an article of faith is the clearest example of this tendency's full flowering. There seems to be little doubt that in the minds of some of the Fathers of the Council this was a proof in the strictest rationalistic sense: that is, a demonstration where no presuppositions are chosen by the one demonstrating, but are rather received in pure passivity from his experience of the manifold and where his conclusions are ineluctible. It would take us far afield to deal with the proper understanding of the Council's definition. Suffice it to say, that within the larger context of theological tradition, the intention of certainly some of the Fathers to "prove God" rationalistically, is simply an untenable interpretation. The statement must be read as saying something like "God's existence is a reasonable conclusion," which is, of course perfectly acceptable and true.

his own various experience. But there is no "over-head reality" by which the mundane can be judged, ready at hand for the men who live in the "one-storyed universe" which Amos Wilder calls the modern world.[53] Out of the welter of experience, man *chooses* his values and his meanings and chiefly by two characteristic acts, both commitments, the act of belief or faith and the act of creative preference. Both of these choices result in an ordering of experience which does not appeal beyond experience for its vindication.[54]

The act of Christian faith asserts, of course, that a transexperiential reality does exist, but claims no warrant for its existence except the experience of faith. "No man has seen God, at anytime."[55] The only revelation of God is as incarnate in his Christ which means within the conditions of experience. ("Philip, you who see me, see the Father.")[56] But Christ, as incarnate God, can only be apprehended in faith. ("Do you not believe that I am the Father and the Father in me?")[57] The experience of faith, as Christianity teaches is, of course, graced — that is, it cannot come to be without an influence from "beyond" experience. God intervenes to "move" us to faith. But that intervention is never detectable in the sense that its presence can be demonstrated even to the one who is subject to it, and certainly not to another "neutral" observer. The supernatural not only builds on the natural as the consecrated theological formula has it, but is never without the natural. One does not aggrandize his fidelity to belief in the supernatural by lessening his regard for the world of natural experience. Every supernatural influence is only known in experience and as experience, which means

[53] Cf. his essay "Art and Theological Meaning," in *The New Orpheus*, ed. Nathan Scott (New York: Sheed and Ward), p. 407.

[54] I do not mean to limit the possibility of ordering choice to these two. The choice of more purely cognitive orders such as we have seen operating in the procedures of scientists, may well be another class of choice all together. An analysis of the similarities and differences among the various acts of choice from which man finds meaning and value in the flow of his experience, would be a long and painstaking task, and it is not mine at the moment. To this question a recent essay by J. Bronowski in *Encounter*, "The Machinery of Nature" (Vol. XXV, No. 5 [Nov. 1965], pp. 45–53), offers some illuminating remarks on the differences between the poetic and the scientific orders which go much deeper, it seems to me, than his treatment of the same material in *Science and Human Values*. Here, I cite the acts of artistic and religious choice as important and enduring stratagems of order which are not exclusively significant to the achievement of value, but are central to such achievement and central, of course, to my interest.

[53] Cf. his essay "Art and Theological Meaning," in *The New Orpheus*, ed. Nathan human being except he be separated from this mortal life," *S.T.*, Ia, q. 12, a. 11.

[56] Jn 14:9.

[57] Jn 14:10.

it is not known as supernatural except as an experience of faith *in* the supernatural and as experience it will have "natural" motivations that seem quite adequate to explain its existence without appeal to the supernatural. The experience of the believer can always be explained away by the nonbeliever at least to the nonbeliever's own satisfaction without involving a transexperiential presence and power. And the believer must submit to this explanation, for within the frame of reference chosen *for*, if not *by*, him, it may well be a perfectly adequate explanation. The man who believes in an immaterial soul does not strengthen his position by thinking less of the body — or by seeking to deny that every act of the soul is accompanied by bodily changes which are explainable according to their own physiological and biological laws.

All of that is a way of saying that the act of Christian commitment and trust in the saving graciousness of God is an act in and of our experience. To make acts of faith, to regard and esteem them, are not ways to retreat into rationalism. They do not provide a toehold in the eternal empyrean. For the transcendent God whom the Christian encounters in his act of faith is always incarnate within that act itself and the act is experienced as a choice. Indeed, what the general intellectual rejection of rationalism has done is to legitimize faith as one of the chief means to achieve a sense of values. Religious belief and commitment are royal roads to morals.

The university has little doubt that its task involves the discrimination of experience as well as its clarification. Although its chief thrust is to provide theories of action for society at large (if you do such, such and such effects will ensue), there are few Dryasdusts who do not recognize that providing theory always implies an intention to set standards. The purely hypothetical is too limited a boundary to the university's sense of its own task. (Doing A is *better* than doing B.) Theory, then, can never be without an hortatory dimension — indeed, as I have argued, pure theory is a cognitive impossibility. It follows that the university must heal the historical traumas which were inflicted on its corporate psyche by an erstwhile arrogant theology, and have resulted in the massive suspicion which still greets the theological enterprise in university circles today. The university *has* to find place for theology, for to continue to disregard it is not merely to disregard a discipline skilled in the methods of modern, nonrationalistic epistemology, as I have argued at length: but it is to scorn the chief means to the perception of flexible and intelligent value systems, namely the rational analysis and exposition of religious faith. The university, in order to fulfill its own task of discriminating among the swarm of experience must foster a strong theology.

Granted that theology should find place in the university, the last point I wish to make concerns the specific place which theology should find. I can come to what I want to say most succinctly by stating that theology is always a language art. The present essay has already argued this conclusion by insisting on the reluctance theology must feel to abstract too far from the personally experienced order of reality, by placing the act of faith within the class of acts of intersubjectivity and by calling attention to the resistant ineffability of mystery; for all of these have tended to the conclusion that the practice of theology is inseparable from the ceaseless task of purifying language.

It is in the nature of all cognition to seek to impose a stasis on the flow of experience. Concept and definition are the substance of all knowledge and they are static. They seek to fix and congeal experienced reality; and in doing so, they in some measure destroy it. Language used conceptually is attempting this cognitive freeze. But language will never be an adequate instrument for fixing and eternalizing experience. Rationalism has always found it a broken reed. A far superior tool for the purposes of pure cognition is mathematics. This is so because, as I remarked before, the mathematical symbol is visual. It states with remarkable clarity and univocity a spatial relationship. It is unthinkable that one could follow a complex mathematical argument without the use of writing. The Euclidean diagrams retain their semantic intention unchanged over the centuries, because the spatial relationships remain identical. But language never attains the semantic serenity of mathematics. It stays closer to experience; and the words which sounded illuminating yesterday are questionable today. For language is more truly expressive of knowing rather than of knowledge, that is, of the experience of cognition which moves continually from light to shadow, from clarity to obscurity.

Language has two dimensions: the semantic and the powerful.[58] The first seeks merely to communicate meaning in disdain of practical concerns or consequences. It is along this first dimension that language

[58] This distinction I borrow from some remarks made by Professor Arthur McGill of Princeton (at the recent consultation on Hermeneutics — Drew University, April 20–23, 1966). Professor McGill is not responsible, of course, for either my understanding or my use of his distinction.

would arrive at a total commitment to the ends of cognition. A semantic intention moves toward mathematics as its expression; and only the incapacity of mathematics, at its present stage of development, to express certain large areas of meaning, prevents our completely abandoning words for serious semantic purposes. For the second dimension of language is always present whenever words are used. Power, creating an effect, moving action — these are intentions present in every use of language. Curses, invocations, paratactic words of all sorts ("Gesundheit" "Marvelous" Drop dead") are examples of language used for explicit purposes of power. But even when the speaker intends to exploit the semantic dimension only, there is a dynamism in language which works against him. Homophones, and puns, portmanteaus, *lapsus linguae,* chance associations, as well as the constant shifting of philological history, all pressure the user of language into continual revision. As T. S. Eliot says in *East Coker:*

> . . . one has only learnt to get the better of words
> For the thing one no longer has to say, or the way in which
> One is no longer disposed to say it. And so each venture
> Is a new beginning, a raid on the inarticulate
> With shabby equipment always deteriorating
> In the general mess of imprecision of feeling
> Undisciplined squads of emotion.

The two dimensions of language are continually at odds. The power of language is often suicidal in the sense that it destroys its own meaning its other half.[59] James Joyce in *Finnegan's Wake* exploits the self-destructive power of words to an unprecedented degree. ("Collidescope," for example, is a sound that can never simply signify the child's toy again for anyone who has read the book.) But what the dimension of power in language destroys time and time again is its own capacity, from its semantic dimension, of serving the exclusive purposes of cognition and so destroying experience. Language is self-destructive of its own power to destroy the experience of mystery.

Oh, it's an imperfect instrument! Strict meaning is better conveyed by diagram, number grids, and equations. Effects come faster and surer from machines, inquisitions and cattle prods. But language remains

---

[59] It should be noted that meaning, the semantic dimension operates against the dimension of power as often as the other way around. The ideal of *poésie pure,* language exploited for the mere effect of vermiculated patterns of sound, is always corrupted by the intrusion of meaning. The semantic demands of language can never be utterly ignored either.

the expressive instrument of imperfect, actual man who is neither seer nor politician, but uncomfortably hesitant between both. And it must be the imperfect instrument of the university scholars who study and explain actual man, the historians, the humanists and those scholars who have undertaken the important task of articulating actual man's faith, the theologians.

III

The Phenomenon of Change
in the Church

BY WILLIAM SCOTT, S.J.

"Everything is the sum of the past and nothing is comprehensible except through its history."

Pierre Teilhard de Chardin

SECTION ONE — CHANGE IN FORM AND STRUCTURE

The present mood of the Church, brought into sharp focus in Vatican II, is a new self-awareness, a reappraisal of her position vis-á-vis the modern world, an acknowledgement that her presentation of Christ and his message to this world has become increasingly meaningless to that world and finally a decision to reform and renew herself so that she may begin again to speak in understandable accents to the men of this time.

Change, then, is the course she has embarked on, and the change to which she has committed herself touches every aspect of her life. Her understanding of herself, her worship of God, her relation to other religious bodies, her involvement with the world and its problems, the role of her members — laity, clergy and hierarchy — these are but some of the major areas into which her decision to change is reaching.

What does all this mean, this decision to change? How is one to understand and appraise this new development? It will help, first of all, to try to grasp the mentality of those responsible for this new way of thinking. George Lindbeck, in his assessment of the new mood, singles out three characteristics of this new mentality. To understand these is to take the first step toward comprehending why the Church is thinking and acting as she presently is:

1. "There is the absolute conviction among those who are forming the mind of the future that the era which began 1500 years ago with Constantine is dead and buried. Never again will the Church dominate culture and society."[1]

2. There is also the conviction that "the church must adapt itself to the contemporary world . . . . This is much more than a reluctant consent to adjustments, to concessions, to the inevitable. . . . No, says the modern Roman Catholic, we must positively accept the modern world. We must stop being nostalgic about the past. God has his reasons for bringing the new order into existence. There is good in it and we must learn from it."[2]

3. "There is a third aspect of this new mentality which is actually basic. By themselves, the openness and eagerness to reform . . . are without content and could lead to sheer modernism of the sort which destroys all historical continuity, whether Christian or Roman. What gives substance to the progressive movements, therefore, is the return to the sources, a return, first of all to the Bible, but also to the fathers and to the liturgy of the first centuries."[3]

What emerges from this characterization as the basic element of the new mentality is a newly rediscovered sense of history. And in the light of this sense of history the Church has been able to move from a position where she viewed herself as a changeless institution, not subject to the changes and deformations that history brings to every human institution, to a position where she has come to learn from a study of

[1] George Lindbeck, "The Thrust of 'Progressive' Catholicism," *Commonweal,* Oct. 18, 1963, p. 106.
[2] *Ibid.,* p. 106.
[3] *Ibid.,* p. 107.

her own history how constant the impact of history has been on her life, her worship, the way she has framed her teaching.[4]

Until very recent years the Church in which we lived was seen as *the* form of the Church, a fixed, immobile structure, unalterable no matter what the changes in the world around her. An image of the Church had developed which tended to identify more and more closely the Church as she exists in history and the final kingdom of God which is to be formed at the end of history. The glory, the changelessness, and the perfection of the latter were attributes that were more and more predicated of the former.

Now Vatican II has come to see that this was an unhistorical view of the Church and her actualization in history. She is a pilgrim Church, on her way but not there yet. Her members are sinful and sinning humans and the modes in which they express her life from age to age will always mirror the imperfections of that membership. And because this is so the Church will always lie under the necessity of reform. The Church in which we lived prior to Vatican II was not *the* form; it was *a* form which the Church had adopted at one point in her history as the best way to meet the needs and challenges of that age. Now the Council has decided that the prior form of life is no longer meeting the challenges of present history and so a new form must be developed. It was the Council's work to begin the building of this new form by developing its blueprint. There remains the task of implementing the blueprint, reducing it to actuality in the life of the Church.

Before going on to consider some of the elements of that new blueprint one further idea on the Church in her relation to history should be noted. History teaches not just the lesson of change but also the lesson of continuity. In reading history the Church must see there the forms and structures, the attitudes and mentality she has assumed throughout the centuries. Yet at the same time it is her task to see how the essentials of her life and message perdure unchanged under the varying historical expressions of those essentials. As Congar sees it, the right study of history will serve this double purpose.

> History is a great teacher of truth. . . . What is wanted is an awareness, in full knowledge of the facts, of the historical di-

---

[4] For a discussion of this "triumphalism" which long characterized the Church's way of thinking and speaking about herself confer "Priests For a New Era," in *Cross Currents*, Summer, 1965, pp. 260–262. Michael Novak treats the same subject in a more extended form in his discussion of non-historical orthodoxy in *The Open Church* (New York: The Macmillan Co., 1962), pp. 52–70.

mension which affects everything existing in this world. We are apt to see not only the mystery of the Church, but all ecclesiastical realities [hierarchy, sacraments, etc.] as if they were supratemporal and for that matter intemporal. That is one of the reasons why we find it so difficult to try to imagine new forms, a new style for these sacred realities; sometimes we even dismiss the attempt as presumptuous and idle. The episcopate, for example, is an institution of divine and apostolic origins; but historically it has taken more than one form and it has been lived in very different styles. Because the episcopate, as authority and as sacrament, is always the same, we are inclined to overlook the gulf that separates the leader of a local community in the early Church, a bishop of feudal times, and a twentieth-century pastor. The Church and the priesthood are of all time; but they are also the Church of today, the priesthood of today. . . . Through familiarity with historical forms we can distinguish more clearly the permanence of the essential and the variation of forms; we can locate the absolute and the relative more exactly, and so better remain true to the absolute while we shape the relative to the needs of the times.[5]

To retain the absolute while shaping the relative to the time, this is the task that the Church has set herself. Let us now apply this kind of historically-aware mentality to an understanding of the present changes occurring within the Church.

In the light of history it is clear that the pre-Vatican II Church was built four hundred years ago in reaction to the Protestant Reformation. Needed at the time to meet a serious crisis in the Church's life, its mentality, attitude toward the world, view of itself, liturgical worship, manner of formulating and teaching doctrine, all these hardened along rigid lines during ensuing centuries. The stance adopted, the mentality developed for that age and that crisis tended to become more and more normative and moved toward becoming the final and definitive structure of the Church. And along with this hardening of the Church's life into only one possible mode of expression there grew up the mentality that saw changelessness as of the essence of the Church. To speak of other possible forms and structures to embody the Church's life was to speak in almost heretical terms.

It is out of this mold of thought and away from its Counter-Reformation embodiment of the Christian life and message that Vatican II has moved. A new Church is on the way to being built. To appreciate

[5] Yves Congar, *Power and Poverty in the Church* (Baltmore: Helicon, 1964), pp. 13–14.

this new structuring and mentality it needs to be seen set side by side and contrasted with the Church it is replacing.

Born out of the need to counter the attack of the Protestant Reformers, the Church of that age came to be characterized by defensiveness. The flock of Christ, in danger from revolt and heresy, needed to be defended. The message of Christ, under attack, came to be projected in terms of a polemic and apologetic theology. Rather than attempt to find in the Gospel message creative ways of meeting contemporary problems, theology tended to a position of defending the Catholic way of viewing things against the position of non-Catholics.

The world, more and more dominated by the hostile spirit of the age, became increasingly a dangerous and evil place. The Christian life, more and more threatened by that world which was successively heretical, deistic, rationalistic, atheistic, and finally secularistic, became progressively a more complete withdrawal from that world. To be a Christian and at the same time to live wholeheartedly in the world seemed to be mutually incompatible vocations.

And to undergird the protectiveness and defensiveness a spirituality of withdrawal developed over the centuries. It was a spirituality that found its classic expression in the *Imitation of Christ,* a world-view that counseled concern for the kingdom of God to come as the one thing necessary. It implied that attention to the things of this world contradicted, or at least distracted from, the Christian vocation. Thus the mentality of protectiveness and defensiveness and the spirituality of withdrawal fed mutually on each other, serving each to buttress the other.

Under another image this flock that needed to be shepherded by its pastors can also be viewed as an army under siege. This image helps to understand two other aspects of this Counter-Reformation Church. If an army is to be successful in its operation, it is essential that authority be exercised in a military fashion: orders must be given and received in a context of unquestioning obedience. Such is the mark of a well-organized army. And this type of exercise of authority came to characterize the relationship between superior and subject in the Church.

Again, essential to the conduct of a successful campaign by any army is the need for a central headquarters. Here overall campaign strategy can be mapped out and then communicated to the generals in the field for execution. And in the Counter-Reformation Church there grew a stronger and stronger central headquarters. Centralization of authority developed in the growth in power and authority of the Roman Curia.

When the Church of the sixteenth century turned to the practical task of reforming what needed reform the attitudes just described tended to express themselves in the reforms adopted. A few examples will illustrate the point. First, there was ample evidence of the need for reform of the clergy. Lack of careful training for the priesthood was evident in widespread ignorance and immorality among the clergy. To reform and defend the ordained priesthood the Council of Trent set up the system of seminary training as we know it today. Candidates for the priesthood were to spend long, careful years of preparation. Heavy emphasis was to be laid during these years of preparation on the study of philosophy and theology. A priestly asceticism was to be taught which stressed the need for careful avoidance of the world as a place of danger. McNally describes the system that was adopted in these words:

> Urban faculties of theology were gradually deserted, for in the post-Tridentine ideal the priest was to be educated in a private seminary rather than at a public university. His priestly training was more moral than intellectual. Ultimately the seminary would move to quiet, pastoral scenes where, secluded from the affairs of men, the seminarians would lead a life disciplined about prayer and study. And though this seclusion from the world distorted the practical, pastoral aspects of their training, it remains almost connatural to sacerdotal education.[6]

This withdrawal for a long period of training from the people they were to serve when ordained developed a distance between priest and laity. They dwelt in totally different worlds. A reform of this type was clearly called for at the time. But the withdrawal was allowed to harden over the centuries into remoteness, and the legacy left to the contemporary Church by this enduring reform has been a real difficulty of communication between cleric and layman. There is a salutary lesson here, as there is indeed in many aspects of the Counter-Reformation Church. The Church can never allow one form to become the final and definitively unchangeable expression of her life. Each age will continue to express its own needs to be served by the Church. And it

[6] Robert McNally, *The Unreformed Church* (New York: Sheed and Ward, 1966), pp. 99–100.

is the need to be served that is paramount for the servant Church, not the preservation of a form.

The order of bishops also came under sharp attack by the Reformers, many of whom saw no scriptural justification for it. It became necessary, then, to defend the role of the bishop and his importance in the Church. Ready to hand for the defense there lay the thousand-year-old alliance between spiritual and secular authority. Many of the trappings of secular rulers had already passed over to the leaders of the Church, and though the secular power of the Church was on the wane and would within a few hundred years die completely the marks of rank and the insignia of importance continued to be attached to the episcopal office. Titles of honor, rings and coats of arms, the episcopal palace, distinctive liturgical garb, all these served to underline the importance of the bishop's rank in the Church. But again the practice adopted by the Church developed into a two-edged sword. For all of these signs of position also came to accent the singularity, the set-apartness of the bishop. The father of the family, shepherd of the flock relation that bound the bishop to his people in the early Church was replaced in the Counter-Reformation Church by one of remoteness and inaccessibility.

To underline the role of ordained priest and bishop against the Reformers' attacks there were also two other instruments available: the liturgy and the manner of expressing the nature of the Church. Both of these became, in the Counter-Reformation Church, expressions in the life and thought of the Church of the distinction and difference between the clergy and the laity. And they also pointed to the active status of the one and the passive status of the other in the Church.

The Liturgy — By the sixteenth century the liturgy had moved a long distance from its original form, even more importantly the respective roles of priest and worshiping community had been drastically altered.[7] Originally quite simple in structure and deriving its elements from the Lord's Last Supper with his apostles, it had been transformed under the cultural pressure of succeeding centuries to the point where by the late Middle Ages it had become a sacred drama, rich in vestment and musical accompaniment, magnificent in its Gothic cathedral setting.

---

[7] The effect of historical circumstances on the development of the liturgy has, within recent years, been extensively studied. One may, for example, read McNally, *op. cit.*, Chap. 1 and 4; or Theodore Westow, *The Variety of Catholic Attitudes* (New York: Herder and Herder, 1963), Chap. 1; or Schall-Wolf, *Current Trends in Theology* (New York: Doubleday, Image Books, 1966), Chap. 5.

At the beginning it was directed to the people, in their tongue and involving their full, active sharing in the worship with their priest in their midst as a father in the center of his family. History had transformed it into a mysterious ritual, offered in an unintelligible tongue, by the priest separated from his community. He stood at the altar sacrificing for them as their representative, and the Christian people stood and knelt in silent awe and adoration at a distance from the altar of sacrifice. As the sixteenth century approached, attempts were made to reform the liturgy and restore its original spirit. But none of the attempts succeeded.

With the coming of the Reformation the mother Church, by one of those strange ironies of history, found the needed reforms being implemented by those who had left her. Central to the program of the Reformers were radical changes in divine worship. They restored the liturgy to the native tongue of the people. Participation of the entire community in the rite was stressed. The Word of God was translated from unknown Latin to known mother tongue, and its proclamation and exposition stood at the heart of the service. The cup was restored to the layman and once again voices were lifted in songs of praise and thanks.

The Church's reaction to this aspect of the Reformation was to remain firmly committed to the expression and accent that the liturgy then had. Looking back through glasses colored by the knowledge and experience of four intervening centuries and at the risk of oversimplification, one can discern at least two aspects of this reaction which, when allowed to harden over the centuries, produced deforming overemphases in the Church's living of the Christian message.

The first aspect of this reaction was that the then existing structure of the liturgy with its insistence on the centrality and importance of the priest provided an ideal instrument for countering the Reformers' insistence on the priesthood of all believers. Where the one side insisted that all men are priests and by deduction from this that there was no need for an ordained priesthood, the other side almost inevitably countered by strongly asserting the importance and distinctness of the ordained priesthood. It has taken four centuries to see that the truth lies in neither extreme position.

The other unfortunate aspect of the reaction was that necessary liturgical reforms became, in the climate of those times, unattainable. Inaugurating reform in the liturgy at that time came too uncomfortably

CARL A. RUDISILL LIBRARY
LENOIR RHYNE COLLEGE

close to capitulation to the Reformation for the contemporary Church to consider it in an objective and realistic sense. Again four centuries were needed to restore the possibility of reform.

Nature of the Church — Along with the liturgy the manner of thinking about the nature of the Church also came to be an instrument for highlighting the importance of the ordained clergy and hierarchy in the Church. There grew up in the post-Reformation Church a tradition of viewing the Church primarily in terms of her organizational structure. Theological treatises laid heavy emphasis on the hierarchic, organized, pyramidal nature of the Church. At the apex of the pyramid in a position of supreme teaching and ruling authority was the Holy Father. Ranked below him in descending order of position and authority were the cardinals, bishops, and priests, and, forming the broad base of the pyramid, the laity.

It was inevitable that this view would imply that the Church is divided into the governing and the governed, the active and the passive members. And underlying this dimension but never explicitly formulated lay the assumption of different degrees of membership in the Church of God. It is evident too that this way of considering the Church found a congenial mode of expression in the way the liturgy continued to be structured with the priest active and the people passive.

Such is the picture of the Church that the Reformation era gave birth to. And the mentality that this Church has made its own makes the cultivation of a sense of history a peculiarly difficult task for the ordinary member of the Church. His whole process of education, the entire cast of his thinking conditions him to view the Church in static terms. This is the Church as she has always been; in fact, the Church as she must be. This is the only form in which she can exist. To suggest to this mentality that the Church could be, and indeed, has been different in past ages and could again change to different forms, structures and mentality is to suggest the unthinkable, the heretical.

Actually, if one views the Church in the context of her two millenia of life, it becomes quite evident that the Church has always known change and adaptation to her environment. The static view that sees her as unchanging is historically untenable. Oddly enough the real conservative is the one who wants to keep the principle of adaptation alive in her, who refuses to betray her history by attempting to introduce the principle of changelessness into her nature.

The tragic element in the two reactions: for and against change, is that they bear witness to the presence in the Church for the past fifty years or more of two diametrically opposed trends of thought. On the one hand, the supreme pontiffs, the professional theologians, the biblical and patristic scholars have been developing a line of thinking aimed at adapting the Church to the contemporary world, calculated to recover from the riches of her past those elements best able to speak to modern man and modern problems. And side by side with this mentality there has continued among the great majority of the priests and lay members of the Church the fostering of the belief that the Church is unchangeable. Church and world must, in the nature of things, go their separate ways. The Church always has been and always will be as she is now.

Between the two mentalities there has been little meeting of minds and hence a rather complete misunderstanding on both sides. No significant effort was developed to set up lines of communication between the two points of view. And then suddenly — for all practical purposes five to seven years is sudden — the climate of change was upon us, bringing a mixture of reaction and a rather general lack of understanding of what was happening.

Were Proctor and Gamble to plan the introduction of a new soap or the American Tobacco Company to contemplate a new cigarette a careful presale campaign would be mounted to highlight the attractive features of the new product and underline the needs of the consumer which it would satisfy. The comparison may be somewhat irreverent but the point it makes is clear. A far more effective communications system was needed. Had there been one, much of the present mixed reaction might have been avoided. It is sobering also to realize that the success or failure of implementing the spirit of Vatican II will likewise hinge on the Church's ability to communicate that spirit in meaningful terms to its members.

At any rate the period of change is upon us and most indications point to its being on the scene for the foreseeable future. The intelligent way to deal with and understand the phenomenon is to set it within the context of its background, to see how it was prepared for, to answer the question: why is this happening, to discover, in a word, a sense of history.

It would not be too much to say that the decision of the Church in Council to change was almost completely predictable in the light

of her history for the past sixty years. At least five areas of the
Church's life and thinking during that period establish this predictability: (1) the development of a social dimension in viewing the
nature of the Church; (2) an unbroken advance in restoring the liturgy
to its full role in the life of the Church; (3) a steadily growing consciousness of the position and responsibility of the layman in the life of the
Church; (4) the constant encouragement by recent popes of a return
to the sources of our faith, the Scriptures and the early Fathers of
the Church, and the application to their study and interpretation of all
the historical and critical tools of modern scholarship; (5) the effect
on the Church, particularly the American Church, of more and more
college-educated members. Other facets of her life could be considered
but each of these has made a significant contribution to the Church's
present idea of herself; together they provide ample proof that the
Church has been consistently building toward the present renewed
understanding of her nature. Together too they disprove the contention that the Church is changeless.

The facts of her recent history make it abundantly clear that she has
at one and the same time been partially implementing change for the
past six or seven decades and also pointing forward toward a more
complete and radical adaptation of herself to the contemporary scene.
The thinking and planning is at least a half century old in its origins.
What we are witnessing is the natural flowering of this into adaptation well thought out and carefully prepared for. The pontificate of
John XXIII, his dramatic calling of the Second Vatican Council and the
series of changes in form and attitude that characterize the present
situation of the Church are not sudden, unexplainable eruptions of
completely unpredictable behavior. They flow from the long and careful
preparation laid down during the five pontificates that preceded John's.

I — *The development of a social dimension* — The pontificate of Leo
XIII (1879–1903) is the transition period from the Church of the nineteenth century to the present Church. It is the hinge that swung the
door of the Church open to the contemporary society.

As a legacy from immediately previous history Leo inherited a
Church closed in on itself and cut off from the world of its time.
Within it the dominant concept of the Christian life was of salvation
attained by each individual through his own personal effort. Each
found his own way to God guided by the commandments and fortified
by the sacraments which provided the strength needed to lead a good

life. Sunday mass afforded the weekly occasion for renewing one's individual contact with God and for storing up the spiritual strength needed to face a world at once hostile and alien for the Christian intent on his quest for salvation. Prayer life was focused on personal devotions and aimed at the same end, a personal relation with a personal God. Life in the Church was structured to provide the best possible assistance to the individual.

It was in this Church that Leo began to speak of the social implications of Christianity. The Church, as he saw it, needed to become concerned with the community of mankind, not primarily nor exclusively with man the individual but with man the social being in his relations with society and with other men. She must engage herself with the problems of the world. It was not enough to counsel resigned acceptance of the will of God to men faced with unemployment, poverty, injustice. A positive program was needed to relieve social ills and rebuild society so that men might live decent, human lives. To this task he dedicated himself; to cooperation in its implementation he called the members of the Church.

A corner was turned. Nineteenth-century individualism began to be set aside to be replaced by insistence on the need for concern for others. One did not find salvation alone. It was to be found with others. Part of Christianity's message was that men had responsibilities one for another. It was in working with other men for the good of all men that the Christian would most surely reach salvation.

By the same movement that set aside overemphasis on the individual nature of salvation to replace it with social concern Leo began to open the door of the Church to the world. The Church of the nineteenth century had been characterized by an attitude of withdrawal from the world. That world, which had been built by rationalism, by the forces of political progress and the discoveries of science, posed a real threat to the living of Christianity. Against it the only course that seemed safe was disengagement. Inside the walls of the Church the Christian could be safe; once he stepped outside the protection it offered he entered a realm of mortal danger for his eternal salvation.

Now Leo began to say that it was not in withdrawal but in engagement that the Christian life was to be lived. No longer were the Church and her members to live lives apart. There must be involvement in the affairs of men. There must be concern for the social good. It was the role of the Church to enter the world, to offer her help, to become engaged in the agonies with which men struggled in their quest for human life.

With Leo, then, two new currents flowed into the mainstream of the Church's life: a swing away from the individual to the social nature of Christianity and the concomitant involvement of the Church in the great problems of mankind. And this was clearly a change from what had been. No one who takes history seriously could affirm that the Church of Leo XIII was the Church of his predecessor Pius IX. It was the same Church and yet quite different in its outlook, in its concerns, in the face it turned to the world. The world called for a different response and with Leo came the beginning of that response. Yet the same history that testifies to the beginning also testifies that it was *only* a beginning. There were some few who took up Leo's vision and began fostering social consciousness and a new look at the Church in the light of that consciousness, but by far the majority of Catholics continued to live in the closed in and closed off Church. Personal piety and personal concern for salvation continued to be the normal expression of Catholicism. The time was not yet ripe for the transmission of the papal forsightedness to the generality of the Church.

II — *The restoration of the liturgy* — Leo's successor Pius X (1903–1914) began the next chapter of preparation for change in the Church, the rediscovery and renewal of her liturgical life. He recognized that the newly reawakened social consciousness of the Church, her renewed sense of the community of all men would find a real source of strength if she could renew her own internal sense of community. To begin renewing this interior life of prayer, of worship and of Eucharist would be to start to move toward the day when the members of the Church would come to recognize that their concern for the problems of their fellowmen was simply the natural consequence of their living a life of community within the Church. Hence, for Pius X the principal emphasis became the renewal of the Church's liturgical life.

With his decree on the frequent reception of the God of love in communion, his enunciation of the basic principles of liturgical renewal, his fostering of good Church music, and his attempt to begin what he saw only a future Church could complete — a thorough reform of the Church's liturgical life — with all of these moves Pius took the first step toward restoring love and community to their central place in the Church. St. Paul's vision that in eating the Body of the Lord Christians thereby became members of that Body and linked intimately to each other was on its way to restoration in the Church's life. But the realization of that vision was still decades away. It would not be until Pius XII's encyclical *Mystici Corporis* that the essentially communal nature of Christ's Church would be firmly reasserted after centuries of dormancy. The same Pope's encyclical *Mediator Dei* in 1948 would carry on the work of Pius X by laying down a solid doctrinal basis for liturgical renewal. But it would take, finally, the documents of Vatican II on the liturgy, on the Church, and on the Church in the modern world to spell out all the social implications of the frequent eating together of the Body of the Lord. But in re-emphasizing the need for love of the eucharistic banquet and for a revivified liturgy Pius X was plowing the field and planting the seed of love and community. Years of germination would follow. We are only today witnessing the flowering of that planting in our recently won realization that the Eucharist commits us to love and therefore to the world, to all men and to all their problems.

III — *The role of the layman* — The next stage in the Church's half century of preparation for the dramatic changes introduced by Vatican II began with Pius XI (1922–1939). With him started the modern Church's concern for setting aside an image of the laity which saw him in an essentially passive role: as member of the flock, the taught, the governed, the base of the pyramid. It came to be seen that such a view of the layman derived from a theology of the Church which was overly juridical and organizational in its emphasis. Now the movement began toward a more scriptural view of the Church. In this view she was seen in more organic terms, as Christ's Mystical Body, the community in and through which Christ lives and acts in the world. And as this thinking came gradually to prevail it was seen concomitantly that it is in each member of his Church that Christ lives and acts. Each (layman, cleric, hierarchy) bears responsibility for the Church's life in his own life and action.

Under the encouragement of Pius XI the apostolate of the laity began to be implemented. The first stirrings of lay involvement in the mission of the Church, his witnessing to the Christian message in the secular world began to appear. Throughout the thirties and forties more and more evidence of lay response to the papal summons continued to appear: the Young Christian Workers, the Catholic Worker movement, the Grail, the Legion of Mary, the Christian Family Movement, labor schools to train leaders for union work, lay edited magazines, Hospitality Houses to care for the poor in the slums of the great cities. The movement had begun which would culminate in the great commitment of the Church to the life and problems of modern man expressed in the *Constitution on the Church in the Modern World* of Vatican II and the same Council's *Decree on the Apostolate of the Laity.*

With the accession of Pius XII (1939–1958) the pace of lay apostolic activity quickened. He laid to rest the active-passive dichotomy in thinking about membership in the Church:

> It would be a misunderstanding of the true nature of the Church and her social character to distinguish in her a purely active element, the ecclesiastical authorities, and on the other hand, a purely passive element, the laity. All the members of the Church . . . are called to collaborate in the building and perfecting of the Mystical Body of Christ. All are free persons and must therefore be active.[8]

He delineated more clearly the precise area of responsibility that belonged to the layman in the mission of the Church:

> [The Church] must today, as never before, live her mission; she must reject more emphatically than ever the false and narrow concept of her spirituality and her inner life which would confine her, blind and mute, in the retirement of the sanctuary. The Church cannot cut herself off, inert in the privacy of her churches, and thus desert her divinely providential mission of forming the complete man, and thereby collaborating without rest in the construction of the solid foundation of society. This mission is for her essential. . . . Under this aspect the faithful and more precisely the laity, are in the front line of the Church's life; through them the Church is the vital principle of human society. Accordingly, they especially must have an ever clearer consciousness not only of belonging to the Church, but of being the Church. . . .[9]

And throughout his pontificate he continued to foster the lay vocation within the Church, describing more sharply the nature of that vocation:

> The relations between the Church and the world demand the presence of lay apostles. The consecration of the world is in its essence the task of laymen, of men who are intimately involved in economic and social life, who take part in government and in legislative assemblies.[10]

[8] Address to Second World Congress of the Apostolate of the Laity, Oct. 5, 1957. For the full text confer *Directives to Lay Apostles* (Boston: St. Paul Editions, 1963), p. 242.

[9] Allocution to College of Cardinals, Feb. 20, 1946; confer *The Lay Apostolate* (Boston: St. Paul Editions, 1960), pp. 641 f.

[10] Address to Second World Congress of Lay Apostolate in Oct. 1957; confer *Directives to Lay Apostles,* p. 244.

And again in even more specific terms:

> One of the most urgent undertakings at the present moment and one which the Church can accomplish above all through the action of the laity is also the inauguration of a truly Christian economic and social world. . . . It is important to consider with particular solicitude the plight of those who are most abandoned and to seek solutions for the crucial problems of our time: a juster distribution of material resources, housing, hygiene, social security, participation in the benefits of culture, a responsible and active presence in the economic field and in public life.[11]

It comes as something of a shock to a mid-sixties Catholic to read such words written ten to twenty years ago. All that he sees as most contemporary in the Church's present concern for the world's problems echoes through a great part of the writing of Pius XII. To one familiar with that writing what is presently occurring is the long overdue reduction of papal pronouncement to concrete and practical implementation.

Yet even in recognizing this movement from thought to action cautious hope rather than optimism is the indicated reaction. It required many years for the thought of Pius to filter down and become the generally accepted thinking of the hierarchy. They, in their turn, have written a concern for the world and an insistence on the active involvement of the laity in carrying out the concrete applications of this concern into the documents of Vatican II. But as yet there is little evidence of the setting up of meaningful and workable channels of communication between laity, clergy and hierarchy which will allow for open, honest exchange of views among all segments of the Church. Until this is done and the wisdom and experience of all is brought to bear on the problems that are of concern to all there is little chance that the layman's part in bringing the Church's message to bear on the problems of the world will be anything more than it has been for centuries, a docile and unquestioning acceptance of a continuing passive role in the Church. Yet if the thought of the past few popes and the decisions of the Council mean what they say there is unquestionably a task in the mission of the Church which can and should be done only by the laity. And it will not be done until the layman is convinced that he has been admitted to active and cooperating partnership in forming the decisions and policy which are to implement papal and conciliar thought.

IV — *Historico-critical study of the sources* — One of the major heri-

[11] *Ibid.*, p. 245.

tages bequeathed to the modern Church by the Counter-Reformation Church and particularly by nineteenth-century Catholicism was a deep suspicion of modern scholarship and its methods. Condemnation of its dangers and warning against its corruptive influences characterized the attitude. The approach to contemporary cultural developments was one of caution and wariness. This world had been built by the children of the Reformation, and so it was flawed in its origins and unorthodox in its development.

During the first few decades of this century Catholic scholars lived in the shadow of this mentality. To complicate the situation the Modernist movement at the turn of the century had provided ample grist for the mill of reaction and withdrawal. These men had shown how far wrong Catholics could go in their attempt to make the faith relevant to modern man. Reaction to the movement only intensified the already prevailing attitude of defensiveness and refusal to enter into dialogue with the contemporary world. Yet like most incidents in history the Modernist controversy produced its good as well as its bad effects. The climate in the Church following its condemnation was a compound of both reaction and prudent advance in scholarship.

> . . . the main influence the modernists had on the two generations of theologians, biblical critics, liturgists and social reformers was negative: they were an example of how *not* to proceed. In this sense the modernists had a good effect, and the same might be said of the fanatical anti-modernists, known as integralists from their insistence on an "integral" Catholicism. For both the heresy and the personal and ideological excesses of the counter-heresy of integralism . . . forced those who would work for a meaningful reconciliation of the Church with modern life and thought to deepen their scholarship, broaden their understanding of, and enthusiasm for, Protestant thought . . . and most importantly, learn those rich difficult languages, clarity, persuasion, humility and delay.[12]

With the accession of Pius XII the slow movement toward openness to contemporary scholarship which had been growing cautiously for several decades came to maturity. His 1943 encyclical on Scripture study, *Divino Afflante Spiritu*, became the Magna Charta of modern Catholic biblical scholarship. The door was opened for scholars to begin taking advantage of all the tools of historical and critical scholarship which Protestant scripture scholars had been developing since the mid-nineteenth century. In consequence of the new openness there developed a

---

[12] John Ratte, "The Spector of Modernism," *Commonweal*, July 23, 1965, p. 533.

new era of biblical, liturgical, and patristic scholarship. And it is this development which has opened up a whole new dimension in Catholic thought, particularly in the area of scripture studies.

Once used as a quarry for proof texts to establish the biblical foundations of the juridical and organizational view of the Church, the Scriptures were now studied in their organic wholeness and were situated in the cultural environment which they reflect. The literary forms used by the different authors, the sense of historical continuity in the story of salvation, the tracing out of themes as they developed from age to age in the Old Testament and came to fulfillment in the New Testament, these were some of the tools used to fashion the new scripturally oriented view of the Church which permeates the documents of Vatican II. It is the same renascence which underlies the recovered insistence on the centrality of the Word of God in the renewed liturgy of the Church.

V — *The effect of higher education on the Church* — The last element that has been part of the climate out of which the present changes are emerging has been the evolving educational status of the layman within the past thirty years. This has been particularly true in the American Church. People who were immigrants and for the most part poorly educated were quite content with the passive role that was theirs in the Counter-Reformation Church. But within the past two generations the percentage of Catholics going on to college and university education has been steadily rising.

Where higher education fulfills its proper function, it produces a questioning and critical mind. Exposure to contemporary philosophy and its insistence on the dignity and inviolability of the human person, realization of the personal freedom and individual responsibility accorded by the social and political structures within which modern man lives, awareness of the lesson of history that all human institutions have been built in response to the needs and demands of particular eras and have either died or moved on to new forms for succeeding ages, all these are the influences that play a part in the formation of educated man.

As a result today's layman tends to be critical of a Church which, he feels, does not come to grips with his present world and its problems; he tends also to want a voice and part in determining how the Church is to meet his own felt needs and those of his society. Paradoxically, the American Catholic Church in its program of higher education has been producing in ever greater numbers in recent years laymen who have grown more and more dissatisfied with the very institution that has provided them with the critical powers without which they would be unable to pass such critical judgement. As Monsignor Ellis describes the situation:

> There has inevitably appeared a closer scrutiny of all that pertains to the Church, a sharper and more critical turn of mind which makes the educated Catholic layman of the second half of the twentieth century a quite different person from his unlettered immigrant grandparents of two or three generations ago.[13]

These, then, are some of the important formative factors that have been at play in the life of the Church for the past half century or more. Out of these elements was produced the Church ready for the Second Vatican Council when it came and prepared to begin with the Council the building of a renewed and restructured Church. Against this background we turn now to the Council itself. We will consider only some of the changes blueprinted by the Council. The word blueprinted is deliberately chosen because the Council has laid down the lines along which the restructuring of the Church is to proceed. But there lies ahead the work of many years, the implementing of this blueprint in specific and detailed changes in liturgy, in relations with other faiths, in the status of the layman in the Church, in the attitude adopted vis à vis the modern world.

THE SECOND VATICAN COUNCIL

I — *The liturgy* — Session One of the Council produced the *Constitution on the liturgy*. The practical implementation of this at the parochial level is perhaps the most concrete evidence of change that the individual Catholic has encountered. That implementation bears witness to another element present in the complex process of effecting change. There has been strong resistance to the change in many quarters, evidencing the continuing presence in the Church of the mentality that views the Church as unchangeable. And underlying this mentality lies the even more basic problem, the failure or inability to communicate a sense of the two thousand year old history of the Church, and particularly of her recently past history, to the members. The lesson is a pointed one. There is urgent need for the development of a sense of history, of process, of change in all segments of the Church. Without it the program of renewal and reform is certain to end at best in uneasy and reluctant

---

[13] John Tracy Ellis, "The Catholic Layman in America Today," *Commonweal*, June 22, 1962, p. 320.

acceptance of what is not at all understood, at worst in the abortive failure of much of what the Church has been working toward for fifty years. Ultimately such failure will mean the continuingly growing inability of the Church to relate meaningfully to the contemporary world.

In the perspective of the history that we have traced out the *Constitution on the Liturgy* is to be seen as the restoration of an active part and voice in the liturgy to the too long silent and inactive members of the Body of Christ. In terms of the Counter-Reformation Church it is the restoration of balance, a correcting of an overemphasis on the ministerial priesthood at the expense of the priesthood of all believers; it is a return to the Christian people of their part in the Church's communal worship of God.

Needed above all is the realization that there is here no change for the sake of change but a return to the wellsprings of Christian faith, the New Testament and the early liturgies that grew out of this. And the return is not a mere love of antiquity for its own sake; it is rather an attempt to recapture and then reexpress in contemporary terms the strong sense of community and attachment to the Eucharist as the love banquet of the people of God which glows so warmly in the pages of the Acts of the Apostles and the letters of St. Paul. Awareness of the communal nature of salvation and the expression of this conviction in all areas of life is the ultimate objective aimed at in the liturgical renewal.

II — *Nature of the Church* — The Third Session of Vatican II saw the promulgation of the *Constitution on the Church*. The language that the document uses to describe the reality of the Church makes it quite clear that the pyramidal, structured, organizational thinking on the Church, developed during the Counter-Reformation, is being replaced by a view which is deeply rooted in Scripture. In this view, the more traditional one in the age of the Fathers of the Church and held for at least the first thousand years of her history, the onesided emphasis on the Church as structure is counter-balanced and completed by an emphasis on her as a living organism. It is a people that the document describes, not an institution. This is the gathered community of God brought together under the Spirit of love into the living Body of Christ. And each in that Body is seen as a living and serving member of the total Christ.

Into this community all enter by the same door, baptism; and once incorporated all are committed to the task of this community, the service of its living Lord which means ultimately the service of the whole Body and the whole race of man. In such an organism what distinguishes the members one from another is not the degree or kind of membership but the manner of serving the Body and the world. And in this connection St. Paul's words in describing the need for the function of each member makes it quite clear that the Body serves its Lord well only when each contributes his own unique service to the whole.

> For the Body is not one member but many. If the foot says, "Because I am not a hand, I am not of the body," is it therefore not of the body? And if the ear says, "Because I am not an eye, I am not of the body," is it therefore not of the body? If the whole body were an eye, where would be the hearing? If the whole body were hearing, where would be the smelling? But as it is, God has set the members, each of them, in the body as he willed. Now if they were all one member, where would the body be? But as it is, there are indeed many members, yet but one body. And the eye cannot say to the hand, "I do not need thy help"; nor again the head to the feet, "I have no need of you." . . . Now you are the body of Christ, member for member" (1 Cor 12:14–27).

To visualize such a concept of the Church, set aside the picture of a pyramid and think rather of a pool of water into which a pebble is dropped and of the series of concentric circles spreading out from that center. The figure makes two points: (1) the vertical image of the pyramid with its suggestion of ranks and degrees, of active and passive, is replaced by a horizontal image suggesting one membership and a basic likeness in belonging. (2) the members of this organism are differentiated from each other not by their manner of belonging but by the kind of service they offer the Body. And there are differing circles of service. All fall inside the outermost circle, and within this circle all are called to service by bearing witness in their lives to what it means to be a Christian. In this service we are all one. As the center is approached, the kind of service offered is differently specified yet all occurs within the community of service. There is the circle of service of those who serve by offering sacrifice and preaching the Word of God, the ministerial priesthood; there are those who serve the community by governing and leading it, the hierarchic priesthood. And at the center there is he who bears as one of his proudest titles, the Servant of the servants of God.

Thus the central thrust of the *Constitution* is toward emphasizing that the Church is a living, active community wherein each serves the needs of all. When this vision of the Church becomes the common possession of all the membership, it can only have extraordinary results in each member's personal spiritual life (other-directed rather than self-regarding), in the community's liturgical life (a common worship to prepare for service of each other), in the manner in which each sees his own vocation within the Body ("I have come not to be served but to serve") and lastly in the attitude adopted with regard to the whole world of men (not withdrawal but service).

III — *Collegiality* — The third basic change in viewing the nature of the Church that was adopted by the Council is contained in the notion of collegiality and its implications. The intent here is to replace the over-centralization and the military exercise of authority characteristic of the Counter-Reformation Church with a decentralization of authority and an exercise of that authority which is familial rather than military.

a) *decentralization* — In its strict theological sense collegiality sees the bishops of the world as responsible not merely for the good of their own dioceses but, in union with the Pope, for the well-being of the total Church. Commenting on Chapter III, article 22 of the *Constitution on the Church* where the notion receives its most extended theological discussion, one commentator points out some of the implications of collegiality in these words:

> All bishops who are united to the Pope and to their fellow bishops by the hierarchical communion . . . constitute a collegial body enjoying supreme power in governing the Church. Such supreme power is exercised not only when the college is united in an Ecumenical Council but also through other forms of "appropriate collegiate action" not yet specified. In the coming years we shall doubtless see many practical applications of this doctrine of collegiality. One important step which has already been taken is the establishment of a world-wide Episcopal Synod, announced by Paul VI in his *motu proprio* of Sept. 15, 1965.[14]

What direction the further practical implementation of this principle of shared responsibility will take in the future is not yet entirely clear. But enough implementation has already occurred to make clear its meaning and indicate that a quite new application of the principle of authority is envisioned within the Church.

i) The creation within the last few years of twenty-seven new cardinals points, for example, in the direction not so much of greater numbers but rather of greater diversity and internationalization, an attempt to expand the cardinalate to include a broader spectrum of representation from

[14] Walter Abbott (ed.) *Documents of Vatican II* (New York: Guild Press, 1966), p. 42.

more diverse areas of the Church's life than has hitherto been true. The point can be made quite clearly by citing but a few of those chosen as cardinals: Maximos IV, Stephen I, and Paul II are all patriarchs of three of the oldest patriarchates in the Eastern Church; Canon Cardijn is founder of the Jocist movement, one of the pioneer forms of the lay apostolate; four members of the Secretariat for Promoting Christian Unity were also included. Thus representatives of three of the most important contemporary concerns of the Church: relationships with the Eastern Churches, the layman's role in the mission of the Church, and the cause of ecumenism are given positions of pre-eminence at the highest level of consultation in the Church.

ii) Pope Paul also turned his attention to introducing collegiality into the Curia, traditionally Roman-based and largely Roman-staffed. Here too the attempt is being made to introduce a broader representation of the Church universal, East and West. In dealing with the matters within their competence also, the various congregations are to be open to the advice and opinion of the regional conferences of bishops. Viewpoints other than Roman and curial are to be sought in formulating answers to the Church's problems because responsibility for these problems is shared by the whole Church.

iii) That the voice of the entire Church may be heard in meeting and solving her problems and needs provisions have also been made for an international synod of bishops, a structure designed to allow the bishops to share responsibility with the Holy Father for the well-being of the whole Church. Three modes of assembling the synod assure flexibility and universality of viewpoint.

First, the general assembly of the synod will be made up of the representatives chosen by each national episcopal conference around the world. Included too are the patriarchs and major archbishops of the Eastern Churches, representatives of the religious orders of men and the cardinals who preside over the crucial congregations. In this form the total Church is widely represented.

Second, for unusual situations requiring a small group, easily convened yet universally representative, there is the extraordinary assembly comprising the patriarchs and major archbishops of the East and the presidents of the national episcopal conferences.

Last of all, the implementation of shared responsibility for the specific problems of particular geographical areas of the Church is guaranteed by the special assemblies of the synod which will allow the convening of representatives from one area of the Church to deal with the special problems of that area.

From these initial implementations of the principle of collegiality it is clear that the Church is now committed to replacing the overly Roman oriented Curia with a form of government more representative than oligarchic in character, a government more internationally based and more committed to the premise that the whole Church must share responsibility for dealing with her needs and problems.

b) familial authority — At the same time as decentralization begins, the exercise of authority will start to move from the military to the familial. The general of an army does not consult the private in arriving at strategic decisions. But the father of a family, before deciding a matter affecting the entire family tries, if he is wise, to solicit the opinion of his wife and children. They discuss; each feels free to speak and out of the exchange a decision is reached. The father still retains his authority. His is the final voice. But the manner of arriving at the exercise of his authority is totally different from that of a general. It is a familial, not military, exercise of authority.

Collegiality or shared responsibility is the application of this type of decision making to the family which is the Church. As the principle begins to be applied at the national and diocesan level, it will mean the setting up of channels of communication by the bishops of each diocese. Structures will be developed to allow for the hearing of the clerical, religious, and lay voices in matters of common concern to all the members of this particular segment of the family of God.

As this application of shared responsibility develops, it should ultimately lead in the direction of the same sort of exchange and mutual assistance at the parish level so that the pastor will devise ways and means to solicit and act on the opinions and advice of his parishioners.

Thus collegiality is intended to effect a major reform in the manner in which the Church exercises her authority. Authority as service and responsibility communally shared are the keynotes of this change which may well turn out to be the most important single reform effected at the level of practical life in the Church.

Many other changes in the Church's life are envisioned and spelled out in the Council documents: the attitude toward relations with the other Christian Churches, with the non-Christian religions, with unbelievers; reforms of the ways in which nuns, brothers, and seminarians are to be readied for their life of service to the Church; realistic appraisal of the world's present problems and how the Church is to cooperate with all men in their solution; growing realization of the responsibilities of service to the Church and the world that only the laity can meet. All these and more are the problems with which the Council has wrestled. Not all of the solutions offered are hard headed and practical enough; many more detailed plans still have to be formed. But at this, the initial stage, what is important is that the Church has over and over again emphasized the general principles under which all the practical solutions that still lie in the future must be grouped. These are simple and only three in number, but they are the heart of the renewal. (1) The Church is a Church of service; (2) The liturgy must create and feed a family to ready it for service; (3) all the Church shares responsibility for living her life and implementing her service.

Section Two — The Development of Doctrine

One final area of the question of change in the Church remains to be dealt with: the possibility of change in the doctrinal teaching of the Church. Here, perhaps more than at any other point, members of the Church tend to become uneasy and fearful when the subject of change in doctrine is even raised for discussion. Though the forms and structures in which the Church lives her life from age to age may change, the doctrine committed to her by Christ and divinely guaranteed against the possibility of being erroneous, cannot and will not change. This is the position that the majority of members take on the notion of change-ability in the doctrine of the Church. Does this attitude too require rethinking? Have current trends of thought in the Church affected the absoluteness of this position also?

Here again an historical understanding of the state of the question can be helpful in fashioning an answer. Against the background of the history of the Church for the past one hundred years the point of the question grows sharper and our present ways of dealing with it come into focus. We will, therefore, discuss the problem of development of doctrine historically as the understanding of and answer to the problem have developed over the past one hundred years. Five stages mark the history of that thought: (1) Newman's *Essay on the Development of Doctrine*; (2) the definition of papal infallibility by the first Vatican Council; (3) Modernism and its aftermath; (4) the contribution of Blondel to the understanding of Tradition; (5) contemporary attempts to deal with the question of change in the doctrinal teaching of the Church.

I — *Cardinal Newman — Essay on the Development of Doctrine*

Modern attempts to deal with the problem of whether or not the Church's doctrinal teaching can change in the course of history began a little over a hundred years ago with the publication in 1845 of Cardinal Newman's study of the evolution of dogma, his *Essay on the Development of Christian Doctrine.*[15] For Newman an objective study of history made it quite clear that there had been change in the Church's teaching throughout the centuries. But the same history also bore witness to the perduring sameness of that teaching throughout the centuries. His objective, therefore, was not to question whether there had been change; this was unquestionable. It was rather to show that Christian revelation had remained identical with the original apostolic deposit of faith throughout its development.

In his demonstration of this identity in change Newman analyzes the two components of the problem, (1) change or development — how does it occur and what factors are involved in producing it? (2) identity or invariability — what is it that guarantees the line of unbroken sameness in Christian revelation from its beginning to his own time?

1) *process of change* — For Newman there are two basic causes for development in doctrine. There is, first, the normal human instinct to strive for an intellectual comprehension and expression of what one believes. This has given rise within Christianity to a gradually developing explicitation of the initial revelation given to the apostles. Slowly over the centuries Christian minds have probed the meaning of the faith and expressed their understanding in dogmatic formulations. Given from the beginning the data of Scripture and the forms of liturgical worship, the Christian intelligence has, by a process of analysis and comparison, of reflection and deduction, built up progressively more explicit formulations of the original revelation.

In addition to this human tendency toward understanding, the development of doctrine also grows out of the challenges that heresy offers to orthodoxy. The heretic proposes erroneous ways of interpreting revelation and by so doing forces the Church to penetrate more deeply into the authentic meaning of the truth she possesses. Thereby she develops a fuller consciousness and a clearer expression of that truth.

These two fundamental sources of doctrinal evolution work out their

---

[15] John Henry Newman, *An Essay on the Development of Christian Doctrine* (Garden City: Doubleday, Image Books, 1960). All citations from the *Essay* are taken from this edition.

effects in the highly complex process of history where many factors are at work shaping the development both through the work of the individual Christian thinker and in the context of the whole surrounding society. In the case of the individual, the process of growth in understanding is an exercise in implicit reasoning. Once one has the faith all the human faculties are brought to bear to unfold one's understanding of it. Growing slowly, this comprehension is fed by the person's individual dispositions, mental habits, moral instincts and by his reaction to the environment which has shaped him. Gradually it is brought to maturity by the need one encounters to defend and communicate his faith. One comes finally to his own coherent synthesis of the faith's meaning.

Concomitantly with the individual's development of his own apprehension and expression of doctrine the process of growth goes on within society too. Here also all the elements of that society are engaged in producing the development of doctrine. Three elements in particular can be discerned at work in society effecting the gradual formulation of dogma.

There is, first of all, the interplay of ideas that goes on within a society. Different individuals fasten on different aspects of an idea and thus develop their own insights into the truth. The clash of conflicting ideas then occurs, and there is criticism of the varying points of view. Through such an interplay of discussion, explanation, and debate all sorts of ideas and opinions are tested and sifted until finally a view is arrived at which reconciles the truth inherent in the clashing ideas and a synthesis is born, incorporating and expressing truth at a new level of depth and clarity. Thus, through the constant repetition of this process in history, growth in knowledge moves forward.

The second factor at play is the milieu within which the idea develops. Here the diversity of nations and peoples and the differing ways of viewing reality that characterize each are the operative notions. A boy grows into a man in a very particular fashion depending on the environment in which the growing takes place. The same is true of the maturing of an idea. Every people in every era views reality from its own perspective and that perspective is a complex of many factors: inheritance from the past, contemporary social structures and attitudes, political and economic realities, philosophical systems, the state of scientific knowledge. The very words used to speak of reality take on their meaning in that total climate of living and of thought. All of these are woven together by any people in any age to produce its angle of viewing the meaning of reality. Different nations in different centuries view and speak of reality in modes different from those of preceding people. Doctrinal formulations feed on all of this and they grow because of it.

Finally, there is the factor of the practical. What is thought must become what is done. Thus, for example, the notion of the worship of God needs to be expressed in living, meaningful forms. And these will vary from place to place and age to age. Particular situations will elicit differing practical expressions of the truth and these in their turn influence the way in which the idea they express is understood.

All of these factors working alone and in interaction upon each other produce the rich and variegated pattern of doctrinal development within the Church. To one who is aware of historical process denial of change, of growth, of evolution is not thinkable.

. . . here below to live is to change and to be perfect is to have changed often.[16]

2) *identity in development* — For all of his awareness of the phenomenon of change in the Church's doctrinal development Newman was also fully aware of the continuing sameness of the revelation underlying all the variations that history introduces into the Church's way of enunciating that divine revelation. Form developed under the impact of history; content remained unchanging. Evolution took place in understanding, not in what was understood. Consciousness of the truth developed but not the truth itself.

Walgrave, in his study of *Newman the Theologian*, indicates that Newman developed three formulae for expressing the identity of revelation within the development of doctrine. Development can be seen as the "passage from implicit profession to formal expression."[17] Or it may be viewed in terms of a later expression of revelation being a more perfect fulfillment of the idea imperfectly contained in a preceding formulation. Last of all, later doctrinal statements can be conceived as "conclusions already present in the preceding propositions."[18]

Whether one takes the three formulae separately or in conjunction, it is clear that Newman views development as a normal and to be expected phenomenon, but it is subject to a norm which guarantees its continuing identity. And that norm is for him the presence of an infallible teach-

---

[16] *Ibid.*, p. 63.
[17] J.-H. Walgrave, *Newman the Theologian* (New York: Sheed and Ward, 1960), p. 244.
[18] *Ibid.*, p. 245.

ing authority in the Church. The same divine Providence that initiates and supports the process of human history and therefore of change also initiates and supports within the Church that which will insure the continuing identity of that which he wants taught by his Church. Thus in the same way that development is to be expected so too is an infallible teaching authority to be expected. They are correlatives.

Authority is then the fundamental and guiding principle in the development of the human understanding of the faith. Human understanding cannot finally be left to its own powers in the development of doctrine. As Newman sees it, the human intelligence tends to subject faith and its meaning totally to reason's dominion, and in so doing it runs the risk of identifying divine revelation with human reason's ability to understand and express it. He saw, in other words, that revelation has a double dimension, one horizontal, the other vertical. On the horizontal level of human history expression may vary from age to age. But always there needs to be present the vertical dimension, God's presence in the formulation guaranteeing that it does in fact speak his message.

These two dimensions work themselves out in a constant interplay through history. But it is always the vertical dimension, the presence of God in the infallible teaching authority, that dominates the final direction and form that the development takes. In his *Essay* Newman sees seven ways in which this interplay works itself out; they are ways too in which the teaching authority is seen to be clearly directing the progress of development. They are not all of equal importance in his eyes, but the teaching authority makes use of all of them in her function of guiding development and keeping it true in its presentation of the apostolic message. Together they represent his effort to present a total picture of how doctrine grows and develops in the living community of the Church.

There is first and most important of all the principle of the preservation of the essential idea. Here the Church applies herself to finding and preserving, at all stages of her existence and under whatever form the idea occurs, the essential idea of her own nature and the nature of her message. Here the Church's consciousness of herself is at work manifesting itself to the world. As Walgrave puts it:

> The Church, in its visible structure and conduct has always produced the same typical impression as the ancient Christian community had on its pagan surroundings. Today, as at its beginning,

it gives to the world around it the impression of a hidden super-situation, magical and fanatical. Just as in the fourth century, it appears today as the catholica, well organized, compact and intolerant, among a coalition of heresies more or less numerous, which ceaselessly change and disintegrate. Today as in the fifth and sixth centuries, it is centred on Rome, confronts great regional schisms, is oppressed in various places by the civil power and is the target of philosophical schools. Newman's meaning is clear enough; it is that the Church's situation and conduct in the world remain unchanged. It always excites the same sympathies and hatreds, gives rise to the same problems and takes up the same attitude to them. This is possible only if the one animating idea persists under all these phenomena, unweakened and incorrupt.[19]

Second, the Church is also perpetually engaged in developing her own internal understanding of herself. Here the emphasis is rather on the introspective gaze she fixes on herself than on the face she turns to the world around her. Over the centuries her principles of life and belief are the constant subjects of her reflective understanding. To grasp the notion of continuity here one must be prepared to see first how she conceives of herself now, and then compare that self-understanding with the one she possessed at the beginning. Identity in the two understandings points to unbroken continuity in the same one self-consciousness.

Third, in the face of continually developing civilization the Church does not remain rigid and unchanging. Within her lies the dynamic power to assimilate into her synthesis of truth whatever of human thought and culture can enrich her possession of that truth. Thus, for example, Aquinas was able to take the philosophy of Aristotle and employ its thought categories in the service of his own exposition of Christian revelation. Or again, the Church has assimilated into her liturgical worship many elements drawn from Judaic liturgical practice. For Newman this ability to assimilate indicates the vigor and independence of the original deposit of faith. It shows itself strong enough to absorb what is of value from its surroundings. And in the process it is always master of the material assimilated, not being transformed into it but converting and adapting to its own uses and purposes. It dominates and uses what it borrows rather than being dominated and changed by it.

Along with growth by addition from outside there is also the process of development that goes on in Christian revelation within itself, what Newman calls logical sequence. Here the Church's possession of the

19 *Ibid.*, pp. 264 f.

faith moves forward and grows by the power of its own reflection, and by analysis it develops further conclusions and explicitations that arise out of this continual process of analysis. The continuity and authenticity of this growth can be judged by comparing later expressions with the original revelation.

> A doctrine, then, professed in its mature years by a philosophy or religion is likely to be a true development, not a corruption, in proportion as it seems to be the *logical* issue of its original teaching.[20]

The fifth form of true development that Newman sees is the anticipation of later clear and definite formulations in the initial deposit of faith.

> Since, when an idea is living, that is, influential and effective, it is sure to develop according to its own nature, and the tendencies, which are carried out in the long run, may under favorable circumstances show themselves early as well as late, and logic is the same in all ages, instances of a development which is to come, though vague and isolated, may occur from the very first, though a lapse of time may be necessary to bring them to perfection. . . . The fact, then, of such early or recurring intimations of tendencies which afterwards are fully realized is a sort of evidence that those later and more systematic fulfillments are only in accordance with the original idea.[21]

The sixth note indicating true development Newman calls "conservative action upon its past." Here he sees that

> a true development . . . (is) one which is conservative of the course of antecedent developments being really those antecedents and something besides them; it is an addition which illustrates, not obscures, corroborates, not corrects, the body of thought from which it proceeds; and this is its characteristic as contrasted with a corruption.[22]

A corruption would be inserted into the course of genuine evolution if a developed doctrine were to reverse the course of preceding development. When it does not, this is a sign that the later flows out of the earlier as a living change.

Last of all, true doctrinal growth is seen to possess a "chronic vigor." Heresy, in the long span of history, is seen as being short lived. Were

---

[20] *Essay, op. cit.*, p. 197.
[21] *Ibid.*, pp. 197 f.
[22] *Ibid.*, p. 201.

the Church's continuing development of primitive revelation to be a false one she would long since have died, for corruption is the prelude to death. That she still lives and grows in her possession of the truth is for Newman the final indication that she has within her a living principle that preserves her in her possession and development of the revelation committed to her care by Christ.

Thus does Newman put together in a synthesis that attempts to do justice to both the two elements, of change and changelessness, in the Church's development of her doctrine. His legacy to the Church's thinking on this problem was the theory that the evolution of dogma is essentially a movement from implicit to explicit understanding of the meaning of revelation, from lesser to greater clarity of expression. Weigel succinctly summarizes Newman's contribution in a sentence.

The unverbalized dimension of revelation under the pressures of history seeks for adequate verbalization.[23]

His theory has exercised a magisterial influence on all thinking on the subject for the past one hundred and twenty years.

II — First Vatican Council — Definition of Papal Infallibility

The next stage in dealing with the problem of doctrinal change was reached in 1870 with the First Vatican Council's definition of papal infallibility. Whereas Newman's concern had been to deal with both elements in the problem of doctrinal evolution, the changing and the changeless, the focus of the Council was on the element of changelessness. Specifically the concern of the Council was to underline one particular aspect of the work of the Spirit in the Church's fulfillment of the teaching role given her by her Lord. It was he who furnished the continuing assurance through her history that she would faithfully preserve and teach the revelation committed to her. That conserving function he exercised in a pre-eminent fashion in the person of Peter's successors, the popes.

To them the Spirit had been promised not "that they might make known new doctrines by his revelation, but rather, that, with his assistance, they might sacredly guard and faithfully explain the revelation handed down by the Apostles and the deposit of faith."[24] The pope, not as an individual person but solely in his role as supreme teacher in

[23] Ibid., p. 16.
[24] Denzinger, # 1836.

the Church, enjoyed the particular assistance of the Spirit. And he enjoys it not as innovator but as preserver.

When he exercises this Spirit-assisted and preserving teaching function under very carefully specified conditions, he cannot err in his teaching. Thus the continuity of the Church in the fulfillment of her mission to preserve divine revelation is safeguarded. In Newman's framework, the truth is preserved unchanging through all the growing awareness of that truth that history brings. And it is the supreme teacher, assisted by the guiding Spirit, who speaks that unchanging truth unerringly.

The Council spelled out in precise terms the strict limits within which this papal prerogative of infallible teaching authority could be exercised.

> The Roman Pontiff, when he speaks *ex cathedra* [i.e. from his apostolic throne], that is when, exercising his function of shepherd and teacher of all Christians, in virtue of his supreme apostolic authority, he defines a doctrine concerning faith or morals which is to be held by the universal Church — thanks to the divine assistance promised to blessed Peter, he enjoys that infallibility which the divine Redeemer wished to confer on his Church for the definition of doctrines of faith or morals.[25]

Basically the definition requires that three conditions must be operative whenever the pope makes use of this power. First of all, he must be teaching in his role as supreme teacher of the Church. Thus his communications with a local Church or the Churches of one country or region do not meet this first condition. Nor does the teaching he might proclaim as the bishop of Rome, for example, or in a talk given to a group of pilgrims or to the members of an international congress fall within the sphere of infallible teaching. Second, he must use language that makes it clear he is exercising his apostolic authority. The intention of teaching with supreme authority and of binding the conscience of all Catholics irrevocably must be made clearly apparent. Last of all, the subject matter on which he is teaching must fall within the limits of his competence. It is only on matters "of faith and morals" that he may speak infallibly. And the meaning of that phrase is to be understood in the light of the use that the Councils and tradition of the Church have made of it. As Gregory Baum puts it:

> A certain popular understanding of this phrase suggests that "faith" stands for divine revelation and "morals" for the entire field of man's moral life. Yet this is false. "Faith and morals" is a classical

25 *Ibid.,* # 1839.

term of conciliar language. Since God's revelation is not handed on to us simply as a body of doctrine but includes norms of life — in other words, since revelation includes *credenda* and *facienda* [things to be believed and things to be done] — it was often referred to as the teaching on faith and morals. . . . Faith and morals, therefore, have to do with the Gospel and its meaning for human life. They do not include all of human wisdom concerning man's moral existence.[26]

One additional qualification of infallible papal teaching authority needs to be added. In his teaching of the Word of God the Holy Father may, at one time, be enunciating the Gospel message; at another time he may be defending or explaining it against false interpretation. The primary area of his teaching authority is the first of these, the announcing of the Gospel, but inevitably attached to this is the defense or explanation of that Gospel by the teaching of other doctrine, the secondary area of his teaching authority.

The Council definition made it clear that papal infallibility is limited to teaching the Gospel of Christ. It did not spell out whether or to what extent the Pope can teach infallibly in the secondary area, doctrines necessary for the defense or explanation of the Gospel. The way in which his teaching authority has been used with regard to this secondary area in the course of the Church's history makes it clear that such teaching has always been limited to what was absolutely necessary in a given set of circumstances to preserve the true meaning of the Gospel.

As envisioned by the conciliar definition it would be the rare occasion that would call for the exercise of papal infallibility. Beyond such extraordinary circumstances there is a broad field of doctrine and discipline where the Pope teaches and where his teaching calls for acceptance and obedience from the faithful members of the Church, but there is no question of his using his infallible teaching prerogative. In the first case his teaching is irreformable; in the second no such note is attached.

The limits of papal infallibility were carefully set by the Council; yet it was not long before a tendency began to manifest itself in the Church of extending this infallible teaching authority to a wider and wider field. More and more indiscriminately the note of infallibility began to be attached to all public papal pronouncements. The careful distinction between authoritative and infallible papal teaching came to be blurred.

The tendency grew of seeing the whole body of ordinary papal teach-

[26] Gregory Baum, "Doctrinal Renewal," *Journal of Ecumenical Studies,* Fall 1965, pp. 389 f.

ing as a fixed body of unchangeable truth. The necessity of flexibility and adaptability in the use of the Church's ordinary teaching power tended to be lost sight of and an air of immutability attached itself more and more firmly to the supreme teaching voice in the Church.

The contribution of Vatican I to the notion of development was a double one. The first contribution was, by deliberate intent, to delimit and carefully circumscribe a specific area of Christian truth which was not subject to the historical process of evolution and change. Within this precisely restricted area there is no room for change. The second contribution was not deliberately intended but was made by subsequent historical circumstances working on this definition. Interpretation of the intent of this definition led to expansion of the field to which it applied and gradually the position gained support that a large portion of papal teaching was to be viewed as an unchanging body of truth.

III — *Modernism and its Aftermath*

At the turn of the century discussion of the question of the development of doctrine entered a new phase. Newman had worked out a formula for reconciling the two elements in the problem, mutability and immutability. Vatican I had focused on the element of immutability. Now exploration of the problem swung more in the direction of investigating the note of mutability. The precise issue raised was how far is the Church to go in incorporating her message into contemporary thought patterns, what is the extent to which the unchanging can be garbed in changing language without having its changelessness affected.

In the late nineteenth century a number of scholars within the Church became concerned with the problem of bringing the Church's teaching, or rather her manner of expressing that teaching, into fruitful contact with modern thought. It was the fear of these men that if the traditional way of presenting Catholicism did not incorporate into itself the insights of the day the result might be to sever the Church from any meaningful relation with modern man and his society. They wanted to face the problems that the thinking of the time posed for the Church's way of understanding and expressing divine revelation.

The movement represented by the work of these men came to be known as Modernism. Basic to the movement was a determination to take account of the contemporary developments of scientific thought, most specifically in the areas of biblical and historical critical methods, and in the light of these developments to aim at a reworking of the manner of presenting Christian truth which would take the fullest possible account of these advances. The movement can best be seen as it was developed in the thinking of two of its chief spokesmen, Alfred Loisy and George Tyrrell.

Alfred Loisy's [1857–1940] chosen field was ecclesiastical history, and under Louis Duchesne he learned the recently developed methods for the critical study of history. With his studies completed he began his life's work: the application of these methods to an objective, historical study of Christianity. That work was shaped by two controlling ideas: the role of history in determining truth and the phenomenon of evolution and change in all things human.

a) *the role of history* — Loisy saw history as ultimately normative in determining truth. All truth, including that of the Christian faith, must be submitted to the judgment of history. It is for the historian to ask: can the truth that Christianity claims to contain be proven in the real order of history? In his pursuit of the answer to this question the scholar must have absolute freedom of inquiry. Authority cannot put limits to what questions he may ask nor can the formulations of doctrine which the Church has developed in her history inhibit his questioning to determine the true facts of history.

As a historian, Loisy saw his task to be the use of the historico-critical tools of his profession to establish the truth or falsity of the words and events expressed in the Scriptures. Once the relation to historical truth of these happenings has been established then it becomes the theologian's task to explicitate their religious meaning. As Loisy himself put it:

If the history of religion is not established by means of historical research, if the biblical tradition, both Jewish and Christian, has not consistency of itself [i.e. as it appears in the light of historical research] then it is not necessary to count on the magisterium of the Church to give this to it.[27]

For Loisy, in a word, it is only the historical method that can establish the truth of history.

b) *the influence of evolution* — Loisy also contended that each age tends to view and express the Christian reality in its own context. Even Jesus, the founder of Christianity, belonged to his age and spoke out of its historical setting. He taught in an atmosphere of expectant Messianism and thus he stressed the imminent coming of the Kingdom of God; in

[27] Cited in Yves Congar, *La Tradition et Les Traditions*, Paris, 1960, p. 265.

the light of that coming Kingdom he called men to repentance, to belief in him as the Messiah and to expectation of salvation through him. It was his intention not so much to speak final truth as to begin a religious movement. When history passed on to the period following his death, that age read his message in its own context and decided that the embodiment of the Kingdom of God for that epoch was the establishment of the Church. Loisy concluded that the preaching of Jesus recorded in the Gospel belonged to the time and situation in which it occurred and each era of history is subject to the same law. Teaching, preaching, doctrinal formulation of belief, are always conditioned in their expression by the climate of the time in which they take place.

Thus for Loisy, Newman's notion that doctrinal development is a passage from the implicitly possessed to the explicitly known is replaced by the view that development means that each age constructs its own expression of the Christian message to meet its own needs and reflect its own understanding of that message. Yet Loisy saw too that this change from age to age occurs within the continuity of the historical process. It is history itself that supplies the link between past and present and not doctrinal statements carried over from one age to another. Reuther puts Loisy's position on this point quite clearly:

> Loisy, as objective historian, drove with conscious deliberation between both the liberal and the orthodox method of bringing about accord between the present believer and the data of belief. The conservative demands that the present faith of the believer must conform to the past data of belief, while the liberal tries to make the past data of belief conform to the present faith of the believer. . . . Loisy insisted on rejecting either of these as anachronisms and unhistorical constructs. He believed the historian must see the past data of faith in its own terms, no matter how unpalatable it may be to his present faith.

> His present faith must not be projected back anachronistically upon past faith. Its connection with past faith exists rather by its place in organic evolution from it. It is the living tissue of history itself that holds together present and past faith. Present faith then becomes a genuine possibility again, by our recognizing it as precisely that; present faith, organically developed out of the past, and related to it by the stream of history, but no longer trying to project itself unhistorically back upon the past.[28]

[28] Rosemary Reuther, "Loisy: History and Commitment," *Continuum*, Summer 1965, p. 163.

Loisy's approach to the problem of development reflects his own major interest — the study of history. He tends to resolve the tension between the changing and the unchanging by absorbing the second element into the first. History is a story of change and hence doctrinal statement, since it occurs in history, will reflect change. But it is one thing to say that dogmatic expression is subject to change and quite another to say that subjection to change is the only dimension that dogmatic expression has. Nor does it suffice to say that historical continuity of itself supplies sufficient explanation of the unchangeability of revelation's message. For this is again to assert that the history of dogma is the total explanation of what dogma is.

The Christian believer is committed to the position that the Christian message although it is historically incarnated in Christ and works itself out in the course of history, is nonetheless in its origin and its final meaning outside the fluctuations of history. There is a vertical as well as a horizontal dimension to revelation. It is in history, but it comes from and leads to God. Hence its final meaning is not comprehensible only in historical terms. That there is a tension between the horizontal and the vertical dimension of revelation is unquestionable. And the tension gives rise to many prickly problems as to how the two dimensions can be dealt with in a way that does full justice to both. Loisy's solution, the choice of the historical dimension as the final resolution of the problem, suffers finally from the defect that any such solution encounters, solving the problem by eliminating one of the essential elements involved in it.

Yet Loisy did make a contribution to the forward movement of the problem. His value was that he recalled to the Church's consciousness the need of taking very seriously the historical expression of divine revelation. It was a salutary and needed reminder at a juncture in the Church's history when the manner of expressing revelation was tending to freeze into a single, and by implication unchangeable, pattern of thought and language.

George Tyrrell [1861–1909], another chief figure in the Modernist movement, also tried to come to terms with the problem of how the Church, in her presentation of doctrine, could speak relevantly to the contemporary age. His central focus in approaching the problem was an exploration of the meaning of revelation in the light of recent religious and philosophical thought: Kantianism, pragmatism, Schleiermacher's religion of feeling and in general the reaction against excessive rationalism in theology that characterized the time. His own particular reaction against rationalism took the form of a gradually growing dissatisfaction with what he considered the inadequacy of the scholastic system in theology in presenting Christian truth to the men of his time.

Tyrrell did not feel that rational expositions and sheerly logical formulations did adequate justice to what revelation was. For him it was not merely a truth communicated to the mind and therefore capable of expression in just intellectual terms. Rather revelation speaks to and is an experience of the total human being. Feelings play a part in experiencing and expressing man's relation to God. Instinct (or perhaps more accurately, the subconscious) also is a component in the religious experience. Indeed revelation is much more a completely vital experience than an experience of the mind alone which can be fully contained in a credal statement meant only for the mind. Actually the mind and its expressions of the truth play a relatively subordinate role in the field of religion. Revelation is more correctly understood as

> an experience, as the complex sense of a dynamic relationship between ourselves and God, composed of feelings and impulses and imaginings. It reverberates in every corner of the soul and leaves its impress everywhere, in the mind, no less than in the heart and will. It is the total complexity of the experience in which God reveals himself or "shows" himself, not as a "fact is revealed in a statement but as a cause is revealed in its effect. He suddenly draws near to the soul and fills it with himself, flooding each spiritual faculty with his own Spirit. . . ."[29]

Because revelation is so much more complex than a communication to the mind and its expression more than just conceptualizing the truth, Tyrrell felt that theology in its expression of revelation would always fall short of being an adequate expression of it; indeed doctrinal expressions may not only be inadequate, they may positively falsify revelation. It is the continuing living experience of the faith within the Church rather than the doctrinal attempts to speak of it which most surely preserves the Church's possession of revelation. As he put it himself in a letter to his friend Baron von Hügel:

> I distinguish sharply between the Christian revelation and the theology that rationalizes and explains it. The former was the work of the inspired era of origins. It is prophetic in form and sense;

[29] Francis O'Connor, "Tyrrell: The Nature of Revelation," *Continuum,* Summer 1965, p. 171.

it involves an idealized reading of history, past and to come. It is, so to say, an inspired construction of things in the interests of religion; a work of inspired imagination, not of reflection and reasoning. It does not develop or change like theology, but is the subject matter of theology. . . .

The whole [of the Christian Creed] has a spiritual value as a construction of Time in relation to Eternity. It gives us the *world* of our religious life. . . . But I do not feel bound to find an independent meaning in each element, or to determine prematurely which elements are of literal and which of purely symbolic value, which is the core of historic fact and which idealization. My faith is in the Truth shadowed by the whole Creed and in the direction it gives to spiritual life — in the Way and the Life and the Truth.[30]

He goes on in the same letter to point out some of the implications of this view for the meaning and value of theology. It is not in the "rational and philosophical" expression of revealed truth that our faith rests but only in the revealed truth itself. The Church is "the guardian of the deposit of revelation" and "her definitions are simply safeguards and protections of revealed truth." But it is necessary to see that "what she says is often absolutely wrong." Yet it is not to what she says that we give assent, rather it is to "the truth in whose defence she says it is revealed, and to that truth alone we owe adhesion."

And he summarizes his view of the relation between doctrinal expression and divine revelation itself in these words:

Theology, of course, develops like any other science. But the Church is no more infallible in it than in any other science. About all of them alike, as also about history, she makes quite fallible affirmations protective of those implicitly revealed truths which are her sole charge and interest. Thus when I say "The sun goes around the earth," I mean "The Scriptures are the Word of God"; for that is all the Church cares about and has any business to care about.[31]

Though Tyrrell rejects the absolute authority of doctrinal statements, he does admit to the existence of a force active within the Church at every stage of her life and this force is constantly at work shaping the authentic interpretation of the meaning of revelation for any age. This is the religious consciousness of the whole community, the *sensus fidelium*. For him this sense includes all the rational, instinctual, emotional

---

[30] J. Lewis May, *Father Tyrrell and the Modernist Movement* (London: Burns, Oates and Washbourne, 1938 (2nd ed.), pp. 218 f.
[31] *Ibid.*, p. 221.

volitional elements spoken of above. Thus its grasp and expression of
revelation will embody all the elements of human experience that need
to be present in the total human experience that revelation is. This
consciousness is created and guided by the Holy Spirit and it can be
safely relied on both to form and to judge the validity of each new
development of the Church's grasp of revelation.

In the light of the inadequacy of any theological explicitation of revelation the Church must continually fight shy of the temptation to freeze
her expression of the meaning of divine revelation into one set of
propositions, or one systematic and unchangeable expression. Precisely
because the meaning of revelation is inexhaustible the need remains ever
present to try again in each age to capture a fuller glimpse of its reality
without ever laying claim to its ultimate expression. There will always
be the revealed truth itself and the present expression of it. The former
is the kernel which lies hidden under the shell of this present formula
which envelops it. The latter is the shell which points to, interprets,
illustrates, and explains the revealed truth while at the same time it
protects and conceals it. Yet finally the Church can rest assured that for
all its inadequacies this progressive expression which both reveals and
hides revelation is under the guidance of the Spirit, who guarantees that
it will as well protect as it will hide and reveal the Christian revelation.

Like Loisy, Tyrrell too seems to have fallen victim to his own viewpoint. In his recognition of the need for incorporating current thought
patterns into the Church's thinking he was, like Loisy, restating what
calls for constant restatement: the Christian message is meant for men
and must therefore constantly seek language that speaks meaningfully
to men. Where he failed was where Loisy failed, in not seeing that
adaptation is not the same as complete surrender. There is an adaptation that successfully incorporates perennially valid truths, and there is
an adaptation which is achieved only at the cost of completely evacuat-
ing the truth to be expressed. Revelation is a total human experience yet
it is ultimately something more and other than human experience. Its
complete subjection to human experience makes it finally man-made; yet
at the core of the Christian faith lies the belief that revelation is not
man-made; it is God-given.

As events turned out, the magisterium of the Church decided that the
attempts of Loisy, Tyrrell and the other modernists to update the expression of revelation were in error. Their embodiments of revelation in

contemporary forms fell short of expressing accurately the reality of that revelation; they ended up, instead, watering down the content of Christianity to make it fit their own thought patterns. In two documents of 1907, the decree *Lamentabili* and the encyclical *Pascendi*, Pius X condemned the movement and by 1910 Modernism as a movement was dead. The final judgment of the Church was that in trying to give proper place to the subjective and the changing element in the explicitation of revelation Modernism tended to underplay the place of the objective, unchanging truth in any doctrinal formulation of revelation.

Not only was the movement condemned but in the wake of the condemnation there sprang up within the Church an attitude of extreme caution and at times overzealous curtailment of any attempt to make use of current scholarly developments. Not just the attempt to incorporate contemporary scholarship into the Church's thinking but the scholarship itself came to be held suspect. Those who held that the problems posed by this new knowledge needed to be met and dealt with were also subject to suspicion and very close control.

Benedict XV in 1914 censured the overcaution and the excessively harsh treatment of the scholars within the Church who went on insisting that modern developments must be confronted, but it was several decades and two World Wars before the Church had sufficiently recovered from the Modernist crisis to turn once again to face the problem of reconciling the two aspects of the question of development of doctrine: the unchanging truth and its changing expression.

IV — *Maurice Blondel's Theory of Tradition*

During the same period as the Modernists were writing Maurice Blondel [1861–1949] was at work on a theory of Tradition which has since his time vied with Newman's as the most generally accepted explanation of doctrinal development among Catholic theologians. In his study of Tradition Blondel proposed to show that the two ways of viewing the nature of Tradition which characterized the thinking of his time were both extreme. A synthesis was needed which would transcend the limitations while incorporating the valid contributions of each of the extreme positions.

There was, on the one hand, extrinsicism which was primarily theological in its stress. It conceived the Christian revelation as a totality of doctrine given once and for all in its entirety at a given point in history to a Church divinely established as the sole authority responsible for the custody and teaching of this revelation. Aside from this double debt to history — owing to it a point of time at which revelation was given and needing it to establish the Church as divinely supported in her teaching authority — revelation owed nothing further to history. The Church's task is to preserve this revelation from contamination by the flow of history. She fulfills this task by committing to her theologians the datum of revelation for development by means of speculation and systematic explanation. This work is done independently of history. Revelation is a closed system which allows no development from without, no influence by history on the Church, which nonetheless lives its life in a historical context. Only from within can development come by way of explicitation ever more clear, by systematization ever more formulated.

Historicism ranged itself at the opposite extreme with an emphasis that was primarily historical. The tendency here was to view history as the only truth. The right was claimed to treat the content of Chrisianity as a pure matter of history. Loisy's view, already discussed, was a typical expression of this position. Since, in this view, much of Christian belief did not conform to historical fact a distinction was introduced between faith, which is a matter of voluntary adhesion to a doctrine, and history, which is the realm of reason and of fact. There was no necessary correlation between these two orders of faith and history. Thus Christian belief is reduced to pure fideism, an acceptance of a body of doctrine on authority alone, without rational justification for this blind act of faith.

Both of these views were for Blondel inadequate expressions of the meaning of Tradition. A total view should seek rather to show that both extreme views have values to contribute to the tradition of the Church. But the values they contribute are not absolutes in themselves. Rather it is only in the service of that tradition which transcends both of them that each can fulfill its purpose.

There are then two points that need to be understood if one is to grasp Blondel's view of tradition: (1) what is the real nature of tradition? and (2) how does it incorporate into its synthesis the real values that history and theology have to contribute?

1) *What is tradition?* Negatively speaking, tradition is not merely a reflection of the past, a simple conservation of the original deposit of faith which it teaches over and over again to succeeding generations. "It is not a transmission, principally oral, of historical facts, of truths

received, of teachings communicated, of consecrated practices and of ancient customs."[32]

Again from a negative point of view, neither the elements which contribute to the formation of tradition nor the truth it expresses are totally in the order of the rational. He rejects as inadequate the view which holds that

> it reports nothing but things said explicitly, prescribed expressly, or done deliberately in the past by men whose considered ideas alone are sought for, and sought as they have formulated them themselves; it furnishes nothing which could not have been or which cannot be translated into written language, nothing which is not immediately and integrally convertible into an intellectual expression.[33]

From a positive point of view tradition "is a preserving power (which is) at the same time conquering; it discovers and formulates truths which the past lived, without being able to articulate them or define them explicitly; it enriches the intellectual patrimony by minting little by little the total deposit and by making it fructify."[34] A brief look at each element in this description will help to clarify his meaning.

It is "a preserving power" — "it knows how to guard from the past not so much the intellectual aspect as the vital reality. . . . Without doubt she bases herself on texts but she also bases herself at the same time and first of all on something other than them, on an experience always in act."[35]

It is "at the same time conquering." Tradition is not dominated by the elements from which it fashions itself — facts from the past, Scripture, theological speculation, contemporary needs, the life of the members of the Church as expressed in their actions — but rather makes use of them all as they serve her purpose, which is to produce a living synthesis of them always applicable to the present. Likewise tradition not only conquers the past, reducing all the elements of its history to the service of itself, but it is also conquering with respect to the future. "As paradoxical as such an affirmation may seem one can maintain that tradition anticipates the future and disposes herself to illumine it by the same effort that she makes to live faithful to the past."[36]

[32] William A. Scott, "The Notion of Tradition in Maurice Blondel," *Theological Studies*, Vol. 27, No. 3 (September, 1966), p. 386.
[33] *Ibid.*, p. 386.
[34] *Ibid.*, p. 387.
[35] *Ibid.*
[36] *Ibid.*

In other words, Tradition is a living ever-present experience which looks to her past, relying on it to supply her with its richness, yet never completely subject to it, teaching men today in a language which they understand and ever facing the future and its needs and problems with serene confidence in her possession of the truth. She is conquering of both the past and the future.

It discovers and formulates truths which the past lived, without being able to articulate them or define them explicitly.

At every moment when the witness of tradition has need of being invoked to resolve the crises of growth of the Christian people, tradition brings to distinct consciousness elements till then retained in the depths of faith and practice, rather than expressed, stated, and reflected. . . . She has nothing to innovate, because she possesses her God and her all, but she must ceaselessly teach us anew, because she makes something pass from the implicitly lived to the explicitly known.[37]

It enriches the intellectual patrimony by minting little by little the total deposit and making it fructify.

For her works whoever lives and thinks as a Christian, as well the saint who perpetuates Jesus among us as the scholar who goes back to the pure sources of revelation, or the philosopher who strives to open the roads of the future, and to prepare for the perpetual giving birth of the Spirit anew. And this diffused work of the members contributes to the health of the body under the direction of the head, who alone, in the unity of a consciousness divinely assisted, arranges and stimulates the progress of this work.[38]

The key in Blondel's thinking here is the concept of interplay between the various elements in the Church, the faithful supplying the Church with data for the construction of its tradition out of the fabric of their actual living and the Church in its turn using this to develop her tradition which she then uses for the enrichment of their lives.

Without the Church, the faithful would not decipher the true writing of God in the Bible and in his soul; but if each faithful did not bring his small contribution to the common life, the organism would not be entirely living and spiritual. The infallible magisterium is the superior guaranty of a function which finds its natural foundation in the concourse of all the forces of each Christian and of the

[37] *Ibid.*, p. 366.
[38] *Ibid.*, p. 388.

entire Christianity: *viribus unitis docet discendo et discit docendo semper.*[39]

Such then is Blondel's notion of Tradition. The second question to which he addressed himself is how this tradition incorporates into itself the real values inherent in the two opposing views of extrinsicism and historicism.

2) *Tradition as a principle of synthesis* — Blondel is careful to stress that both facts and systems have their own contribution to make to the tradition of the Church, that there is always need of careful historical investigation, and that theological syntheses are indispensably important. But neither the one nor the other, indeed no single element in her life, is the be-all and the end-all of the Church's existence. Neither the one nor the other is the sole or the dominant constitutive of Tradition. The Church relies on them, needs their data, will always use and respect their competence. But their role is ancillary, subsidiary, contributory always, and never dominating or exclusive of the other. For there is "something of the Church [which] escapes scientific control; and it is that which without ever dispensing with or neglecting them controls all the contributions of exegesis and history; for she has in the very tradition which constitutes her, another means of knowing her author, of participating in His life, of binding fact to dogma and of justifying the foundation and the additions of ecclesiastical teaching."[40]

The capital notion of tradition is the Church living her life. She is a living organism, a body, and hence always in action; she lives in the collective lives of her members, and she has need of living her life in order to come to ever deeper and fuller understanding of the truth entrusted to her. "To pass from facts to dogma, the most exact analysis of texts and the effort of individual thought is not enough. There is need of the mediation of the collective life and the slow progressive work of Christian tradition."[41]

All the elements of the Christian Church, all the members of the Body, have their contributions to make to the life of the Body. Each one's work is important; each one's contribution to the general welfare is needed. But for the gathering together of all the elements, for the synthesizing and unifying of every contribution and all action, God has provided the Church with tradition. "The principle of synthesis is

[39] *Ibid.*, p. 389.
[40] *Ibid.*, p. 397.
[41] *Ibid.*

neither in the facts nor in the ideas alone; it is in tradition, which resumes in itself the data of history, the effort of reason, and the accumulated experience of faithful action."[42]

Certainly, history has much of value to offer the Church, and the formulations of theological speculation are of immense service to her, but neither is the total view. Each takes a particular stand vis-à-vis the Church and because it does it sees the Church only from that angle. But what the Church is cannot be seen from any single side. She must be seen from every side. Nay more, she must be entered into; one must live his life in her, the "believing society." Then one comes to see her as she sees herself, always alive, always in act, always becoming more conscious of what she is and has.

Each side, history and dogma, must bring itself to see that if left to itself as the sole norm of truth, it can only give a false, because incomplete picture of the Christian reality. Blondel is sharp in his condemnation of both extremes. Of extrinsicism he says:

> The supernatural does not consist, as the extrinsicist thesis implies, in a relation of notions determined and imposed by God, without there being between nature and supernature any other link than an ideal juxtaposition of elements which are heterogeneous and even impenetrable by one another, between which our intellectual obedience makes the connection, so that the supernatural subsists only if it remains extrinsic to the natural and if it is proposed from the outside like something whose whole interest resides in the fact that it is a supernature.[43]

He is equally critical of historicism:

> Will one have remedied [the extrinsicist position] by offering as the foundation for the temple of souls all the sediment accumulated by centuries of human thought? What can one say of all these stratifications without homogeneity, if not that they bury Christ under debris which is said to be fecund but which is really only like dead leaves.[44]

The values of both need to be preserved but they can only be used as they should be by the unifying force of tradition.

> There can be no final separation of historical conclusions, of ecclesiastical definitions and pious practices, each order, critical science, theological speculation, moral asceticism, evolving apart.

[42] *Ibid.*
[43] *Ibid.*, p. 398.
[44] *Ibid.*

Rather, it is necessary to say that the problem consists in taking them in their real interdependence to determine the original contribution of each, its relative autonomy, and its compensatory action with regard to the others, so that their legitimate independence, the condition of their useful concurrence, is constituted by their very solidarity, and that to wish to isolate the science of the facts or of Christian dogmas from the science of the Christian life would be, while tearing out the heart of the spouse, to ask her to go on living and living for her spouse.[45]

And this unification of all elements into a single life corresponds to the real order of actual living. The Church is not an abstraction. It is a vital living reality, and out of its total living experience it produces its tradition.

One feels by the practice of Christianity that its dogmas have been drawn from reality. One does not, therefore, have the right to place facts on one side and theological data on the other, without returning to those sources of life and action where there is the indivisible synthesis of which the facts and the formulas have been only a double and faithful translation in different language. . . . Between dogmatizing and exegesis there is a knowledge, a true knowledge of action, capable of disengaging for the profit of an experimental and progressive theology the lessons drawn from history by life.[46]

Thus finally for Blondel tradition is the unification of all elements of the Church's life including but by no means exclusively relying on the contributions of either history or theology. It synthesizes into the unity of a single life the total richness inherent in the manifold components of two thousand years of life.

V — Contemporary Thinking on Development of Doctrine

By the 1940's the shock of reaction caused by the Modernist crisis had died down sufficiently to allow the theologians again to direct their attention to the problem of change and changelessness in the development of the Church's teaching.

One of the first to address himself to the problem was Henri Bouillard in 1941.[47] For him every expression of the truth reflects the age in which that expression is made. It is historically condi-

---

[45] Ibid.
[46] Ibid., p. 399.
[47] Henri Bouillard, Conversion et Grace Chez S. Thomas D'Aquin (Paris: Aubier, 1941), pp. 219–224.

tioned. Divine revelation itself, however, speaks of God and hence of inexhaustible truth. Thus the final meaning of revelation cannot be totally captured in the concepts and propositions of any given time. And this tension between the divine truth to be expressed and the human attempts to formulate it will always be present in the Church. Her task is to recognize that what God has committed to her is unchangeable truth. And he has given her the guarantee that it is his truth she will perennially teach. Yet she must equally recognize that she will never fathom the whole of that truth. Rather she needs to give herself in every age to the constantly recurring task of incarnating that divine truth in ways suitable for the speaking of God's Word to that age in meaningful terms. Thus with regard to the truth the Church will always live under tension, the tension of preserving the deposit of faith and at the same time adapting it to the contemporary. She does not fulfill her mission of witnessing God's Word to the world by emphasizing either element in the tension. Her task and therefore the assisting help the Spirit gives her are both directed to the same end: preservation of revelation combined with acceptance of the responsibility that lies on those who have the truth to speak the truth in understandable language.

For Bouillard the "affirmations" of the Church are unchangeable, but her "representations" of the truth are necessarily changeable. The Church must never allow herself to be enslaved by one mode of representing her affirmations, e.g., canonization of Aristotelian concepts as the only valid way of expressing divine revelation. She cannot become the captive of the philosophical preoccupations of any age. Yet she must view her presentation of truth, her theology, as part of the living stream of human thought and expression. The danger of relativism, of complete accommodation to the contemporary is always a real one but its threat cannot keep her from the attempt to speak relevantly to the men of this or any age. And her final reliance in this task of accommodation is the guarantee of her founder that he will assist her in preserving the truth.

Bouillard's position has become, with individual nuances added by each theologian, the basic position of contemporary Catholic thinkers. Hans Küng, for example, points out that a careful distinction must be made between the one faith and its various expressions.

> The distinction between faith and formulation of faith is of fundamental importance. . . . The faith can be the same and the formu-

lations different, indeed contradictory. Behind such formulations of faith stand different ideas and mental images, concepts judgements, and conclusions, and different forms of perception, feeling, thinking, volition, speaking, describing, acting, different forms of consciousness of existence and of the objective world, different physiological, psychological, aesthetic, linguistic, logical, ethnological, historical, ideological, philosophical and religious presuppositions different individual and collective experiences, languages, world views, environmental structures, conception of human nature, and the different traditions of individual peoples, the theological schools, of the universities, and of the Orders.[48]

This distinction ought not to be wondered at, for even in the New Testament Jesus Christ the same yesterday, today and forever is variously spoken of by the inspired writers. St. Paul's view of Christ and his Body, the Church, is quite different from the portrait Matthew or Mark drew of the same Christ. Christ meant different things to different sacred writers; yet it was the same Christ they preached and wrote about.

> . . . in being transmitted the message of Jesus from the beginning . . . was being interpreted, expounded, explained to suit the respective conditions under which the proclamation took place, with different emphasis or attenuations, additions or deletions.[49]

But for all the difference,

> in the writings of the New Testament . . . the exclusive concern was with the primary attestation of God's historically unique act of salvation in Jesus Christ. . . . The proclamation and doctrine of the Church despite all its progress, must remain with Jesus, with the revelation of God promulgated for all time. Every formulation of the faith by the Church must acknowledge that.[50]

Küng's conclusion is that faith and its expression cannot be identified. Rather all those who possess the faith and write of its content must recognize "the imperfection, the incompleteness, and the fragmentary character of their formulations of the faith."[51] For him as for Bouillard no formulation captures the whole truth but the constant striving for significant expression of the truth keeps the Church open to the needs of men and enables her, in an inflexible adherence to God's Word, to create flexible presentations of that Word.

[48] Hans Küng, *Structures of the Church* (New York: Thomas Nelson and Sons, 1964), pp. 385–388.
[49] *Ibid.*, p. 389.
[50] *Ibid.*, p. 388.
[51] *Ibid.*

Thus the obligation of the Church is a twofold one, preservation of the truth from adulteration and openness with regard to differing expression of that faith. She will fulfill that obligation as long as there are constantly present in her consciousness the two realities: the faith delivered to the apostles,

the original apostolic proclamation and doctrine, the testimony of eyewitnesses, appointed by Jesus Christ himself, of his work, his death and his resurrection is the standard for all later proclamation and teaching.[52]

and the doctrinal definition of that faith,

as human — and as historical formulations — the definitions of the Church are inherently capable and in need of improvement.[53]

And the second of these realities is always the servant of the first. Expression exists to serve faith and the validity of any expression needs always to be judged in terms of how well it expresses that faith. It is always a question in judging formulations of the faith

of whether a new development is or is not in keeping with the revelation which has been promulgated once and for all time. It does not suffice for this new development to be neutral from the point of view of revelation; it has positively to affirm it. And much more, too, is it a question of whether the subordination of a new utterance on this revelation, promulgated once and for all time, is real and unquestionable. No popular piety and no *sensus fidelium* can procure a new revelation for the Church.[54]

Karl Rahner, in his treatment of the development of doctrine, sees that development as influenced and effected by a complexus of factors. First of all and dominating the whole process there are the two interrelated realities of the Spirit and the faith of the Church. Both are in the Church, at once possessed by her and shaping her. And when the Church is at work developing her reflexive awareness of the truth she possesses they are operative in the process by which she develops her consciousness.

The light of faith, the impulse of the Spirit. . . . They are the brightness which illuminates the object of faith, the horizon within which it is contained, the mysterious sympathy with which it is understood, and not properly the object directly regarded, not a sun

---

[52] *Ibid.*, p. 389.
[53] *Ibid.*, p. 389.
[54] *Ibid.*, p. 391.

which we can immediately contemplate. But they are present and take part in the apprehension and unfolding of the object of faith; they form the co-operating subjectivity (God's and caused by God) with which the Word is for the first time understood in the act of hearing and understood ever new. Knowledge in faith takes place in the power of the Spirit of God, while at the same time that Spirit is the concrete reality believed: Spirit of the Father and of the Son, Spirit of the Crucified and Ascended, Spirit of the Church and earnest of eternal life, Spirit of justification, holiness and freedom from sin and death.[55]

There is secondly the official teaching magisterium of the Church. That authority holds a special responsibility for development and yet it needs to recognize that its responsibility is exercised and development is achieved through dialogue with the other segments of the Church. It must listen to the other voices and movements in the Church and incorporate their insights into its own growing consciousness of the meaning of revelation.

Third, it is necessary to realize that the Church's grasp of the deposit of faith develops in a variety of ways. Because one normal way of growth in knowledge is by the use of words and concepts there will always be a rational dimension in the development. This growth by understanding may be by way of the explicitation of what is formally implicit in a single proposition of revelation.

When the explicitation is that of a single proposition contained in original Revelation, and when this explicitation only states more expressly ("in other words"), in a different conceptual language, (etc.) "the same thing" as the original proposition (of course with the guarantee of the magisterium that the new proposition correctly renders the sense of the old), there can be no doubt that the new proposition too states what God has revealed.[56]

Again knowledge may grow by "the explicitation of what is 'virtually' implicit in a proposition with the help of another proposition."[57] Here "new knowledge is derived in this properly deductive way as a conclusion from several previously given propositions."[58] But beyond development by such logical procedures Rahner feels there is another means by which the Church grows in her possession of the truth. A proposition need not always be the beginning of such growth. A young man, for

[55] Karl Rahner, *Theological Investigations*, Vol. I (Baltimore: Helicon, 1961), p. 51.
[56] *Ibid.*, pp. 57 f.
[57] *Ibid.*, p. 58.
[58] *Ibid.*, p. 59.

example, who is in love is in the grips of "an experience which trans-
forms his whole being." Conscious of his state though he is, he is unable
to express its full reality in words. From the beginning he grasps a
reality and in that sense "knows" it; but only subsequently, upon reflection, is he able to give more and more adequate expression to what it is
he is experiencing.

> In this progressive self-achievement, in which love comprehends
> itself more and more, in which it goes on to state something "about"
> itself and comprehends its own nature more clearly, the love itself
> becomes ordered; it has an increasing understanding of what must
> properly be the foundation of its own activity, mirrors its own na-
> ture with increasing clarity, approaches as its goal, with an increas-
> ingly clear awareness, what it always has been.[59]

This coming to fuller and fuller awareness of what it means to love
is an experience and a conclusion which is reached through means which
are certainly not just intellectual reflection. The whole person contributes
to the growing ability to express what is possessed.

In the Church's growth in her reflective awareness of a dogma revealed by God a kind of development analogous to the natural one just
described can be discerned. Rahner sees the apostles as initially having
had just such a "global experience" as the state of being in love.

> Christ, as the living link between God and the world, whom they
> have seen with their eyes and touched with their hands, is the
> objective content of an experience which is more elemental and
> concentrated, simpler and yet richer than the individual propositions
> coined in an attempt to express this experience — an attempt which
> can in principle never be finally successful.[60]

Their experience of Christ had inherent in it elements which, though
aware of, they could not articulate. And all of these elements formed
part of Christ's original revelation. The Church has gone on growing
in her explicit grasp of these elements and yet the explicitation is not
just logical. In living her life the Church has come to know what has
always been possessed, as the lover comes to know the meaning of the
love present to him from the beginning.

In the unfolding of this process in the Church's consciousness throughout her history it is evident that the fuller, deeper awareness that arises
out of the continuing reflection comes not merely from the Church act-

[59] *Ibid.*, p. 64.
[60] *Ibid.*, p. 65.

ing as "an historian or a philosopher of religion." Rather she comes to that awareness in the light of faith, "in real possession of the object of faith and in real contact with it through grace."[61]

The work of theology, of intellectual "rumination," is important in this process but it is not ultimately and solely normative in determining the development. The Church's "living, growing, as it were instinctive, awareness in faith" is likewise not of itself enough. Rather

> it is only when the Church, after consideration of some "new" proposition, knows herself to be in definitive possession of the truth, and declares this explicitly and with binding force for the awareness in faith of her individual members, that the just balance of the two aspects in any given case is finally guaranteed.[62]

The past five years have given rise to yet another stage in the study of doctrinal development. Vatican Council II has introduced into the Church a general climate of renewal and reform and traditional patterns of life and thought are being subjected to critical re-appraisal. One has only to read through the documents of Vatican II to become aware that many of the traditional ways of speaking about Christian truths are being replaced by formulations of these truths which are quite different from the explanations which have been taught in the Church for centuries. The citation of but a few examples from among many which might be cited will help to underline how far reaching is the current of change in thinking that is running through the Church.

1) In his first encyclical *Mirari Vos* issued in 1832 Gregory XVI had these words to say about human freedom of conscience:

> From this poisoned source of Indifferentism ["the fatal opinion . . . that the soul's eternal salvation can be obtained by any kind of profession of faith provided that morals conform to justice and probity"] flows the false and absurd maxim or rather madness, that every individual should be given and guaranteed freedom of conscience, that most contagious of errors.[63]

Contrast these words with the following taken from Vatican II's *Declaration on Religious Freedom.*

> This Vatican Synod declares that the human person has a right to religious freedom. This freedom means that all men are to be immune from coercion on the part of individuals or of social groups

---

[61] *Ibid.*, p. 76.
[62] *Ibid.*, p. 77.
[63] Cited in "The Legacy of Pio Nono," by Daniel Callahan, *The Critic,* Oct.-Nov., 1965, p. 32.

and of any human power, in such wise that in matters religious no one is to be forced to act in a manner contrary to his own beliefs. Nor is anyone to be restrained from acting in accordance with his own beliefs, whether privately or publicly, whether alone or in association with others, within due limits.[64]

2) In the area of human morality surely the most evident example of development is the present situation of the Church's teaching on birth control. Ordinary Catholics and competent moral theologians alike have for a long time believed that the Church's absolute prohibition of any form of artificial contraception is unchangeable teaching. Yet recent years have witnessed a growing questioning of this position. The present urgency of the problem of a rapidly expanding world population along with a re-evaluation of the meaning of the natural law theory have, together with other considerations, led to the demand for a fundamental re-thinking of the Church's thinking on this subject.[65]

3) A third and perhaps equally dramatic shift in the Church's thinking and acting has occurred in her relations with the Protestant Churches. Until quite recently the ecumenical movement for a Catholic meant the movement for the return of the Protestant Churches to the mother Church, Roman Catholicism. The climate of ecumenism is now quite different. There is recognized the need for admission, by all parties to the continuing separation, of guilt for both the initial split and the sins of uncharity that have characterized the division over the centuries. All likewise admit that the first step toward ultimate reunion is the sustained effort and reform and renewal within one's own communion. From this beginning the movement toward reunion proceeds to the sincere effort to understand clearly and sympathetically the meaning of the Christian message as interpreted by the other communions. Only then will it be possible to come to grips in charity with the issues that still divide Christians. The Holy Spirit will ultimately achieve the reunion in a way and at a time that is still hidden from human eyes. All that Christians can do is offer him their human efforts toward that goal, leaving to him to make of those efforts what he will.

These and other instances of the Church's changed view on many issues affecting her life and her thought have brought theologians to question whether the traditionally held view of the Church moving from the implicitly possessed truth to the more and more explicitly com-

[64] *Documents of Vatican II*, pp. 678 f.
[65] The present state of thinking on this subject is well summed up in *Christian Morality Today* by Charles Curran (Notre Dame: Fides, 1966), Chap. 4–6.

prehended truth is adequate to explain what is presently happening in the Church. Examples such as the ones cited seem to warrant the conclusion that in some areas of her teaching, at least, the Church has admitted to error in her past position and has moved to substantially new positions. The problem then is to work out a theory of doctrinal development adequate to explain the above and other instances of change in the Church's thinking.

One sympathetic Protestant theologian brings the question to sharp focus in these words:

> We come to the real question when we ask whether the dogma of the Church is also subject to the influence of historical variation. Does dogma stand alone as the one unchangeable and untouched rock within the waves of history, transcending the law of changeability? Or does dogma participate in the law of historical change? Currently, as they have never done before, Catholic answers to this question suggest that even dogma does not altogether escape subjection to time. The forms in which faith is expressed manifest many idiomatic characteristics of their time.[66]

This question of how to account for teaching which is clearly not a more explicit statement of previously held positions but rather a quite different view than previously held has only very recently begun to be dealt with, and the theologians are still searching out the most promising lines along which the answer is to be sought. Thus there has not yet been time for a consensus to develop. This being so, all that can be attempted here is a sampling of the ways in which the problem is being approached by the theologians. It is still too early to predict how the issue will finally be resolved.

Gregory Baum, writing in the *Journal of Ecumenical Studies,* feels that recent doctrinal reforms in the Church make it clear that "understanding doctrinal renewal of the Church simply in terms of development is inadequate."[67] He feels rather that what the Church goes through in passing from one position to another, for example the passage from condemnation to approval of religious liberty, is a conversion experience. The Church is, in such instances, mirroring in her thought the experience that is the basic ingredient in the Christian message and the fundamental meaning of the Christian life. For every Christian life is a passover existence, an exodus out of sin and error into the

---

[66] G. C. Berkouwer, *The Second Vatican Council and the New Catholicism* (Grand Rapids: Eerdmans Publishing Co., 1965), p. 58.

[67] Baum, *op. cit.,* p. 377.

freedom of life shared in Christ; it is a death/resurrection experience, a dying to self in order to live to God. Put another way each Christian life and the life of the Church herself must be an identification with the life of Christ; and his life is a death/resurrection. This is the theme that is present in all of Christian spirituality, in liturgy, in sacramental life.

In her setting aside of one view and her adopting of a new one the Church is reproducing this experience in her teaching. Her possession of the truth must be subject to the same law that governs all Christian growth. She must be prepared, in the face of the developing demands of history, to admit error, insufficiency, incompleteness in her view, set it aside and accept a position more responsive to the present exigencies.

> Must we not admit that it [the evolution of the magisterium] included an element of passover, of dying to the past and living to a new truth, of a passage from error to truth?[68]

Baum makes it clear that the process he is describing occurs in the area of the Church's non-infallible, authoritative teaching. We must relearn to delimit clearly the restricted area of infallible teaching and outside of that area develop the ability to recognize when there is need for change from inadequate to adequate, and at times from erroneous to truthful positions. The development of such an attitude of willingness to reform will demand concomitantly the cultivation of

> humility, willingness to learn from God, and readiness to abandon past positions when we see their inadequacy and to accept deeper truth from the Spirit.[69]

In his view what is called for is a more nuanced and realistic view of the role of the Spirit in guiding the Church. The Spirit is assuredly at work seeing to it that the Church teaches the Gospel infallibly but beyond that she is, as all human institutions are, subject to fallibility, blindness, to poorly developed tools for unearthing the truth, in a word, to all the limitations that being part of human history imposes on all things human. The final summary of the implications of his position is put this way:

> In the area of Christian doctrine, doctrinal renewal is a quest for deeper insights into, and fresh formulation of, the Gospel of salvation which would be in greater conformity with God's Word and

[68] *Ibid.*
[69] *Ibid.*, pp. 377 f.

at the same time be closer to the needs of men today. . . . In the area of natural morality renewal would mean greater sensitivity to real or objective values and a greater awareness of the changes in man himself, that is of the deeper layers of his personality that are being discovered in our age. In the . . . area of biblical and theological research, the reform of teaching implies an assimilation of the progress which the various sciences have made in our day.[70]

Baum's contribution, then, is to acknowledge that error and inadequacy and hence need to change are part of the Church's history of doctrinal teaching. He goes on to suggest that this phenomenon is explainable by an application to the Church's teaching function of the basic Christian themes of conversion and death/resurrection.

Noonan approaches the problem from the same perspective of history.[71] He too finds historical evidence pointing to change in the Church's teaching. This admitted, the question to which he addresses himself is: what explanation ought to be given of the phenomenon of change, especially in cases where the exercise of the Church's infallible teaching authority seems to be involved.

For the practical working out of his own proposed explanation he takes the specific case of the Church's teaching on usury. Prior to the middle of the fifteenth century the Church taught that it was sinful to make profit on money loaned. Not only was the practice condemned as seriously sinful but a considerable body of evidence can be amassed from the writings of the Fathers of the Church, from the pronouncements of the Popes, from the decrees of the Councils of the Church, and from the interpretations given at that time to Scripture's words on the practice to warrant the conclusion that the Church put the full weight of her doctrinal authority behind the condemnation.

Yet within about one hundred and fifty years' time the moral theologians were able to construct counter-arguments which so undermined the Church's position that by the seventeenth century the legitimacy of usury came to be universally acceptable. The example is usury, but the process is observable in other areas of the Church's teaching too. Hence though Noonan's proposed explanation touches directly the case usury [and by analogy the teaching on contraception] it can usefully be applied to other instances of the same process of change.

Noonan sees three explanations as possible to explain this kind of

[70] *Ibid.*, p. 378.
[71] John T. Noonan, Jr., "Authority, Usury and Contraception," *Cross Currents*, Winter, 1966, pp. 55–79.

change. The first explanation would conclude that, since a strong case can be made out for holding that the Church believed she was exercising her infallible teaching authority in the initial position she adopted [usury is sinful], it is legitimate to conclude that in changing her view she was admitting not just that she was fallible in this case but that her teaching in general is subject to fallibility. Thus the conclusion would be that an infallible teaching authority does not exist in the Church. Noonan, however, believes that two other explanations of the situation are possible.

The second explanation would make the point that despite the Church's strong condemnation of usury there was always a considerable number of members of the Church who refused to accept the condemnation, found ways around it and felt justified in practicing usury. The existence of this body of the faithful constituted a limit on the Church's ability to speak infallibly. This view would contend that the Church's power to teach infallibly is limited to those areas which the Church as a whole believes and accepts. Here then the *sensus fidelium* would be seen as determining the extent of infallible teaching authority. Noonan puts his finger on the weakness of this position: "This approach, it may be felt, runs too much the risk of making moral law in the Church depend on democratic adhesion."[72] On this principle the whole range of the Church's moral teaching might be questioned, based on the contention that one could find among Catholics opposition to a wide variety of her moral teachings: abortion, divorce, the just war, etc. This explanation would seem to point finally toward complete subjectivism in morality.

Noonan's own preference is for the third explanation of change in the Church's teaching. The view begins by asking the question: what was the purpose of this particular teaching of the Church? What were her reasons, the values she was intending to protect? For example, in the Church's original prohibition of usury Noonan sees her insisting on the need of justice and charity among Christians. In the economy of the time banning the taking of interest on loans kept the rich from exploiting the poor encouraged the sharing of wealth, and guaranteed "the proper distribution of capital for the life of the community."[73]

As the structure of the economy changed, it was possible to achieve all these ends by different means. Differing circumstances pointed to dif-

---

[72] *Ibid.*, p. 72.
[73] *Ibid.*

fering means for the preservation of the values sought. In consequence of these historical changes the Church's view on usury shifted and she came to approve of interest bearing loans. Noonan explains the change and the implications of that change in these words:

> The proclamation of the Gospel necessarily involves the teaching of justice and charity. But what acts are just and charitable depends on the concrete circumstances of the society. If the economy changes, the requirements of justice and charity will change; some acts will receive more moral emphasis, others less; the moral attitude toward certain activities will be altered; the rules prescribing certain acts and proscribing others will undergo re-examination. What has been thought to have been essential may be seen as essential only in a given context. Such re-examination occurred with respect to the usury rule. The purpose of the rule, to guide men in economic transactions with each other to love each other, was better realized by a new rule, and the absolute prohibition of usury in the old sense was effectively rewritten by the theologians from 1450 to 1600. [This] approach explained how this was possible without error by the Church.[74]

What Noonan is saying then is that the moral legislation of the Church is always intended to preserve certain values that are of the essence of the Christian message, e.g., justice and charity. It had been true and will continue to be true that teaching which guaranteed the presence of these values in one age will not assure their presence in another age; or another age may find better means for the implementation of these values. Thus what he is proposing is that in the teaching of the Church two elements need to be distinguished. There is first the body of perennially valid Christian truths and values. These remain present in continuity throughout the Church's history. But there is secondly the question of how best to incarnate and embody these perduring truths in succeeding cultures and civilizations. Embodiments appropriate to one age may well become meaningless to another age. When this happens, the Church ought to develop new formulations for making her truths present and meaningful to the contemporary age. There is in the Church both the perennially true and the changing embodiment of truth. That the Church will always preserve the message of Christ in this context means that she will always incorporate in her teaching the truths that her Founder committed to her; it does not mean that she is irrevocably bound to one way of expressing those truths; nor does it

[74] *Ibid.*, p. 73.

mean that she cannot be in error if she does not re-interpret and re-phrase her expressions of those truths to meet the changing demands of history.

Baum points out the need for admitting error and inadequacy. Noonan indicates how a proper understanding of her own history will provide the Church with the insight needed to comprehend what her preservation from error in teaching does and does not mean. Michael Novak, in his book *The Open Church*, adds another dimension to the present discussion of doctrinal development. His contention, and there are others who share his view, is that the Church is not well equipped to handle the problem of doctrinal development because she has committed herself too unreservedly to one way of expressing the Christian truth. She is limited in her formulations of revelation to the Aristotelian-Thomistic system of viewing reality. Thus, for example, in describing the presence of Christ in the Eucharist she makes use of the categories of substance and accidents; or again, in speaking of Christ, who and what he is, use is made of the notions of person and nature. Through much of her teaching there runs an almost exclusive reliance on this philosophical system to provide the structures of thought within which revelation will be taught.

Novak's point is that it is not possible to capture within any one system of thought all the richness of reality and all the complexity of revelation. All that one system can hope to do is express partially and from one perspective the meaning of Christianity; but it certainly cannot hope to exhaust its meaning. Specifically, he finds four weaknesses in the method of expressing the Christian message to which the Church has rather exclusively committed herself.

> There are four chief weaknesses which many in the Church have contracted from too long an association with non-historical ortho-doxy. These are: an uncritical use of abstractions; the loss of honesty and candor; an undue admiration for uniformity, with a lack of esteem for diversity; and a blindness to the spiritual values promoted in the secular world. All these weaknesses are related. Love for abstractions discourages personal insight and authenticity. Lack of personal insight favors safe generalizations rather than honesty in specifics. Tepid devotion to honesty leads then to stress on public conformity rather than on individual differences. The remoteness of ecclesiastical abstractions from actual life does not favor a just appreciation for the characteristic values of secular civilization.[75]

[75] Novak, *op. cit.*, p. 349.

His own suggestion is the opening up of the Church's thinking to other than the traditionally scholastic point of view. Room should be provided to include contemporary philosophies and their approaches to reality. There should be movement away from the tendency so strong in recent centuries to look upon the formulations of doctrinal teaching achieved within the Thomistic system of metaphysics as being the most nearly perfect expression of revelation that the human mind can achieve. The cultivation of diversity of approach in expressing the content of Christianity, he feels, can only profit the Church. Unity in the possession of the truth need not imply uniformity in expressing that possession.

It is at this point that we reach the frontier edge of the discussion. Already there are signs of the direction which future development will take. Let the mere mention of three items, two books and a lengthy article, which have appeared recently both terminate this survey and point the future direction. Eugene Fontinell in an article in *Cross Currents*,[76] after leveling strong criticism at the philosophical bases of traditional doctrinal statements, essays an attempt to indicate how Christian belief might be formulated if contemporary philosophical thinking were used as a foundation. Charles Curran, in his book *Christian Morality Today*,[77] begins the application to moral theology of present-day insights. By so doing he introduces a quite new dimension into the present discussion of moral problems. Lastly Leslie Dewart[78] projects an interpretation of the meaning of Christianity which lies quite outside the thought patterns that have characterized theological development for the past few centuries. The direction ahead seems quite clear. There will continue to be attempts to reformulate the Christian faith in terms that are perhaps more meaningful to contemporary man than the traditional Thomistic categories we have been accustomed to for many hundreds of years.

VI — *Evaluation*

The clear trend in the Church's thinking on doctrinal development over the past three or four decades has been in the direction of concentration on the phenomenon of change. This represents a shift in emphasis; the concentration in recent centuries had been rather on the

---

[76] Eugene Fontinell, "Reflections on Faith and Metaphysics," *Cross Currents*, Winter, 1966, pp. 15–40.

[77] Curran, *op. cit.*

[78] Leslie Dewart *The Future of Belief* (New York: Herder and Herder, 1966).

phenomenon of changelessness. Thus what is occurring is a marked change in attitude in dealing with the problem of doctrinal development.

In the midst of this changing mentality there are several basic principles that need to be strongly asserted. They can provide the stability so necessary in a period of change.

1) The first of these is the continuing affirmation of belief in the presence and activity of the Spirit in the life of the Church. He was present and operative in the centuries preceding our own; he is present now. The Spirit was not given for any one age or any one climate of thought. He was given for the duration of the Church's life. That presence then is as guaranteed for a period of change as it is for periods of stability.

2) The past century has witnessed a growing awareness of how important history is in understanding anything human. In the case of divine revelation there is a human and therefore a historical dimension. Men and the Church herself have spoken of divine revelation at different time, in different cultural environments, using different languages and varied thought patterns. And men and the Church have lived the faith in multiformed ways. To accept this is to accept reality. If the Christian faith is not afraid of truth it has no reason to fear history. Careful and continuing concern for the historical dimension of Christian revelation ought to and will be a major emphasis within the Church in the future.

3) Yet there is that in the Church which continues to provide the bulwark against history as the only determinant of the truth and that is the infallible teaching authority. The present situation would seem to call for greater openness, for more willing acceptance of the tentative and the experimental in dealing with the formulation of divine truth. In the final analysis the magisterium is the guarantee the member of the Church has for his possession of the truth. And he can be as assured of that possession by a magisterium open to culturally and historically conditioned formulations of the deposit of faith as by one which has in recent centuries tended to commit herself to only one way of formulating that deposit.

4) Last of all there is need to recognize that the Church is guaranteed the Spirit for the fulfillment of her mission. That mission is the witnessing of Christ's message to men. It is when she is most concerned with speaking that Word in accents that meet and answer man's needs that she is most faithful to her task. It is in giving Christ to men that she can most surely rely on the assisting Spirit. The attempt to speak to

men of this time or any time in language he understands is her surest way to ensure the presence and assistance of the Spirit in her midst.

Conclusion

This brief historical survey is meant only to indicate that the phenomenon of change within the Church, in her forms and structures, in her mentality, in her ways of expressing traditional truths is present to the contemporary Church as it has not been present for hundreds of years. And it will be present for a long time to come. It would not, in fact, be too much to say that the Church for the foreseeable future will be characterized by a continuous process of change, of experimentation, of diversity in almost every area of her life and thought.

What needs stressing and provides stability faced with this prospect is to see that this mentality is very clearly *the* mentality of the present Church. If there is one place in the Church where the guiding activity of the Holy Spirit is most obviously at work and most clearly discernible, it is among the bishops of the whole world gathered together in general council to consider the present and blueprint the future state of the Church. And at Vatican II the need for development of the Church's doctrine to meet the changed needs of this age is a stress present from John XXIII's opening address, to the end of the Council.

At the beginning John said:

> . . . the authentic doctrine . . . should be studied and expounded through the methods of research and through the literary forms of modern thought. The substance of the ancient doctrine of the deposit of faith is one thing, and the way in which it is presented is another. And it is the latter that must be taken into great consideration. . . .[79]

And in closing the Council Paul VI made it clear that the Church is not of one age. She is of the past, of the present, and of the future, and her most pressing task at this moment in history is to contribute to the future not just of herself but of the whole world.[80]

At both the beginning and the end of the Council the two keys to an understanding of the present Church are touched on: her sense of history and her concomitant concern for being contemporary to every age of man. It is the guidance of the Holy Spirit that is responsible for this emphasis.

[79] Abbott, *op. cit.*, p. 715.
[80] *Ibid.*, p. 728 ff.

Index

Abelard, difficulties with ecclesiastical authorities, 19, 21
Acceptance, as verification, 84 ff
American Catholic laity, present dissatisfaction, 111 f
Animism, 53 ff
Apostolate of laity, forms of, 107
Aquinas, St. Thomas, 19, 23 n, 26, 46 n; synthesis of Christian faith, 86
Aristotelianism, 25, 31, 33, 34, 74, 86
Aristotle, *The Organum*, 28
Arius, 24, 68
Arnold, Matthew, 76
Auden, W. H., *For the Time Being*, 59
Augustine, St., 69
Authoritarianism, in theology, 53

Bacon, Francis, 81; naïve optimism, 26; *Novum Organum*, 27; view of scientific knowledge, 83
Barfield, Owen, 80
Baum, Gregory, contribution to theology of doctrinal development, 151; de-

limiting area of infallible teaching, 150; meaning of "faith and morals," 126 f; role of Spirit in Church, 150; summary of views, 150 f; view of development, 149 f
Belloc, Hilaire, 80
Bentham, Jeremy, 41
Bergson, Henri, intellect and life, 70
Berkouwer, G. C., doctrinal change, 149
Bernard, St., and Abelard, 21
Birth control, rethinking of Church's position, 148
Blondel, Maurice, definition of tradition, 137; extrinsicism and historicism inadequate, 136; extrinsicism, an extreme view of tradition, 135 f; historicism, an extreme view of tradition, 136; theory of tradition, 135 ff; tradition, a conquering power, 137; tradition, its discovery and formulation, 138; tradition, final definition, 141; tradition, the gathering of the elements, 139; tradition, and intellectual pat-

159